BLOOM
Founded by | arihant

Olympiad ACE

A Comprehensive Practice Book

for School Olympiads & Talent Search Exams

SOCIAL STUDIES

Class 5

by
Adhishree Neurgaonkar

Olympiad ACE

BLOOM

Bloom Cap Edu Ventures Pvt. Ltd.

Administrative & Production Office

'Ramchhaya' 4577/15, Agarwal Road, Darya Ganj, New Delhi -110002
Tele: 011- 47630600, 43518550

PRICE : ₹125.00

Published by Arihant Publications (I) Ltd.

For further information about the books log on to
www.bloomcap.org

Follow us on

Preface

"Future belongs to those Who prepares for it today"

School Olympiads are National & International level competitions conducted by different Government, Non-Government & Educational Organisations with the purpose of making the children ready to face competitive exams.

The challenging Questions asked in Olympiads motivate them to learn more & more and bring out the best results with improved academic performance. The Awards & Scholarship offered by Olympiads motivate children to aspire & strive for doing better and emerge out to be the best.

Social Studies Olympiads

Social Studies provides students with a comprehensive understanding of society, politics, economics and history. Studying Social Studies helps students understand the complexities of society, and prepares them for careers in fields such as public service, education, law, journalism, and research.

Social Studies Olympiads are meant to develop students' interest towards this vital subject.

'Bloom Social Studies Olympiad Study Book Class 5' is a perfect resource to Study & Practice for Olympiad Exams and other National & State Level Talent Search Exams & Other Competitions.

Some Special Features of Bloom Social Studies Olympiad Study Books are;

- Complete coverage of all the aspects of History, Geography and Civics.
- Chapterwise Exercises having different types of Objective Questions at par with the Olympiad Level.
- Olympiad Pattern Practice Sets at the end.

This book is prepared by Expert Panel with the utmost care, still if you have any suggestions regarding its improvement then feel free to contact us at support@bloomcap.org. We will try to inculcate your suggestions in the further editions.

Contents

01

The Earth

MCQs 1 Mark Questions

1. **The Earth's shape is not perfect circle. Instead what is the shape of the Earth?**
(a) Spherical with flat poles
(b) Spherical with flat at equator
(c) Both (a) and (b)
(d) None of these

2. **The Central longitude that divides the Earth into the Eastern hemisphere and the Western hemisphere is known as ....**
(a) International Dateline
(b) Prime Meridian
(c) Equator
(d) None of these

3. **What is the movement of the Earth around the Sun on a fixed path or orbit called?**
(a) Motion (b) Rotation (c) Revolution (d) None of these

4. **How many days, the Earth takes to complete one revolution?**
(a) 465 days (b) $365\frac{1}{4}$ days (c) $265\frac{1}{2}$ days (d) 366 days

5. **The Prime Meridian passed through which of the following cities?**
(a) London
(b) New York
(c) Greenwich
(d) Dubai

6. **The Indian Standard Time is how much ahead of the Greenwich Mean Time?**
(a) 2 hours (b) 3 hours (c) 5 hours (d) $5\frac{1}{2}$ hours

7. **What are squares called which are formed by the Latitudes and the Longitudes intersecting each other?**
(a) Grid system (b) Grid (c) Pole (d) None of these

8. **Which of the following is the longest latitude?**
(a) Tropic of Cancer
(b) Tropic of Capricorn
(c) Equator
(d) Arctic Circle

9. **Complete the given analogy.**
Green : Plains : : ? : Highlands and Mountains
(a) Yellow (b) Brown (c) Dark Green (d) Red

10. **How mountains prevent cold and hot winds?**
(a) By act as a barrier (b) By blocking the various air masses
(c) Both (a) and (b) (d) None of these

11. **Which of the following features was/were show in physical map?**
(a) Mountains and plains (b) Landforms
(c) States and its Capital (d) All of these

12. **Different landforms such as mountains, plateau and plains vary in elevation and ....**
(a) range (b) altitude (c) slope (d) deposition

13. **Which of the following planets has spectacular ring system?**
(a) Venus (b) Uranus (c) Saturn (d) Neptune

14. **Which among the following is the largest continent of the world?**
(a) Asia (b) Africa (c) Europe (d) North America

15. **Complete the given analogy with regards to flow of river.**
First Stage : Canyons :: Second Stage : ?
(a) Valleys (b) Waterfalls (c) Meanders (d) Rapids

16. **............... is separated from Northern Canada by the Baffin Bay and Davis Strait.**
(a) North Pole (b) USA (c) Greenland (d) None of these

17. **What type of energy is generated using the tool as shown in the picture given below?**

(a) Wind energy (b) Solar energy (c) Hydro energy (d) All of these

18. Which of the following is/are a hill station(s) in Saudi Arabia?

(a) Al Taif (b) Abha

(c) Both (a) and (b) (d) None of these

19. Identify inexhaustible source(s) of energy from the given options.

(a) Sun (b) Coal

(c) Petroleum (d) All of these

MCQs 2 Marks Questions

20. Identify the incorrectly matched pair.

(a) International Dateline – 80° longitude

(b) Arctic Circle – $66\frac{1}{2}$° N

(c) South Pole – 90° S

(d) Prime Meridian – 0°

21. Which of the following statements is/are correct ?

I. Tropic of Cancer passes through eight Indian states.

II. Antarctica is the smallest continent of the world.

Codes

(a) Only I (b) Only II

(c) Both I and II (d) None of these

22. Read the given statements and select which ones are true (T) and which ones are false (F).

I. Latitudes lines runs parallel to each other.

II. The exact location of a place can be known with value of latitude only.

Codes

	I	II		I	II
(a)	T	F	(b)	F	T
(c)	F	F	(d)	T	T

23. Identify the lines from the information given below.

- **These lines runs from the North Pole to the South Pole.**
- **These lines are equal in length.**

(a) Imaginary Line (b) Longitude

(c) Latitude (d) All of these

24. Read the given information and answer the following question.

I am a visual representation of the Earth on a flat surface. I can be considered as one of the oldest forms of communication. Who am I?

(a) Map (b) Globe (c) Earth (d) All of these

25. Unscramble the group of letters to find out the name of the place with the help of information given below.

It gives an idea about the location of continents and countries

Codes

(a) SREESHPEMIH (b) UAQOTER

(c) ROONTITA (d) None of these

26. Match the following.

List I (Continent)	List II (Name of the Grassland)
A. North America	1. Downs
B. Australia	2. Pampas
C. South Africa	3. Prairies
D. South America	4. Velds

Codes

	A	B	C	D		A	B	C	D
(a)	1	2	3	4	(b)	4	3	2	1
(c)	3	1	4	2	(d)	2	4	1	3

Darken your choice with HB Pencil

1.	ⓐ ⓑ ⓒ ⓓ	6.	ⓐ ⓑ ⓒ ⓓ	11.	ⓐ ⓑ ⓒ ⓓ	16.	ⓐ ⓑ ⓒ ⓓ	21.	ⓐ ⓑ ⓒ ⓓ	26.	ⓐ ⓑ ⓒ ⓓ
2.	ⓐ ⓑ ⓒ ⓓ	7.	ⓐ ⓑ ⓒ ⓓ	12.	ⓐ ⓑ ⓒ ⓓ	17.	ⓐ ⓑ ⓒ ⓓ	22.	ⓐ ⓑ ⓒ ⓓ		
3.	ⓐ ⓑ ⓒ ⓓ	8.	ⓐ ⓑ ⓒ ⓓ	13.	ⓐ ⓑ ⓒ ⓓ	18.	ⓐ ⓑ ⓒ ⓓ	23.	ⓐ ⓑ ⓒ ⓓ		
4.	ⓐ ⓑ ⓒ ⓓ	9.	ⓐ ⓑ ⓒ ⓓ	14.	ⓐ ⓑ ⓒ ⓓ	19.	ⓐ ⓑ ⓒ ⓓ	24.	ⓐ ⓑ ⓒ ⓓ		
5.	ⓐ ⓑ ⓒ ⓓ	10.	ⓐ ⓑ ⓒ ⓓ	15.	ⓐ ⓑ ⓒ ⓓ	20.	ⓐ ⓑ ⓒ ⓓ	25.	ⓐ ⓑ ⓒ ⓓ		

02

Our Environment

MCQs 1 Mark Questions

1. **What do you understand by the term Biosphere?**
   (a) Rocks and minerals (b) Plants and animals
   (c) Water resources (d) Lithosphere

2. **The Ozone layer is present in which of the following layers?**
   (a) Thermosphere (b) Stratosphere (c) Troposphere (d) Mesosphere

3. **........ is the uppermost layer of the atmosphere.**
   (a) Ionosphere (b) Troposphere (c) Lithosphere (d) Exosphere

4. **Which among the following gases is/are most responsible for global warming?**
   (a) Carbon Dioxide (b) Water Vapour
   (c) Nitrogen (d) All of these

5. **What is the percentage of nitrogen in the atmosphere?**
   (a) 21% (b) 0.5% (c) 78% (d) 48%

6. **Which of the following is not a Greenhouse gas?**
   (a) Carbon dioxide (b) Methane
   (c) Nitrous oxides (d) Carbon monoxides

7. **How is air pollution caused?**
   (a) By smoke from the factories and vehicles
   (b) By deforestation
   (c) By excessive use of pesticides.
   (d) Both (a) and (b)

8. **Among the given pollutants, which is a secondary pollutant?**
   (a) Carbon monoxides (b) Smog
   (c) Carbon dioxide (d) Fly ash

9. Which of the following does not contribute to pollution in aquatic bodies?

(a) Heavy metals (b) Ozone (c) Microplastics (d) Pesticides

10. Refer to the given list of environmental components in the box and answer the following question.

Plants, Animals, Fungi, Bacteria, Land

The items given in the box are .... components.

(a) Biotic (b) Abiotic
(c) Both (a) and (b) (d) None of these

11. .... is caused when harmful gases released by burning of fossil fuels mixed with water and atmosphere.

(a) Air pollution (b) Acid rain (c) Deforestation (d) Global Warming

12. Which of the following is a method of waste disposal?

(a) Landfill (b) Dumping
(c) Composting (d) All of these

13. .... is measured on Richter scale.

(a) Magnitude of flood (b) Magnitude of earthquake
(c) Volcano (d) Tsunami

14. Why coastal states like Andhra Pradesh and Odisha often face natural disaster?

(a) Due to cyclones (b) Due to landslides
(c) Due to earthquakes (d) Due to floods

15. .... is a sudden violent shaking of the ground and is caused due to sudden tectonic plate movement.

(a) Volcano (b) Earthquake
(c) Tsunami (d) Cyclone

16. What is the mass movement of rock, debris or Earth down the slope called?

(a) Volcano (b) Earthquake
(c) Flood (d) Landslide

17. Complete the given analogy.

Drought : Deficiency of rainfall : : ? : Excess precipitation

(a) Volcano (b) Earthquake
(c) Tsunami (d) Landslide

18. **Identify the process in which people move to cities and towns to live and work instead of the countryside.**

(a) Industrialisation (b) Urbanisation
(c) Migration (d) None of these

MCQs 2 Marks Questions

19. **Read the given information and identify the type of waste.**

- **I decompose easily.**
- **I am eco-friendly and get mixed with soil.**

(a) Organic waste (b) Inorganic waste
(c) Biodegradable waste (d) Non-biodegradable waste

20. **Read the given statements and select which ones are true (T) and which ones are false (F).**

I. Cyclones are violent storms that cause damage in the coastal areas.
II. A hill of mountain with an opening or a vent is called Tsunami.

Codes

	I	II		I	II
(a)	T	T	(b)	F	F
(c)	T	F	(d)	F	T

21. **Arrange the following gases in decreasing order of their percentage in atmosphere.**

I. Oxygen **II. Carbon Dioxide** **III. Nitrogen**

Codes

(a) I, II, III (b) III, I, II
(c) I, III, II (d) II, III, I

22. **Select the incorrect statement(s) about pollution.**

I. Water pollution is major cause for acid rain.
II. Water pollution harms marine life.

Codes

(a) Only I (b) Only II (c) Both I and II (d) Neither I nor II

23. **Unscramble the letters in the given options and select the one that is not a cause for soil pollution.**

(a) CRACKERRIFE (b) PESTIDICE
(c) ERUNAM (d) None of these

24. Match the following.

List I	List II
A. Water pollution	1. Factory dump
B. Air pollution	2. Forest fires
C. Noise pollution	3. Machines
D. Soil pollution	4. Chemicals

Codes

	A	B	C	D		A	B	C	D
(a)	1	2	3	4	(b)	4	3	2	1
(c)	3	1	4	2	(d)	2	4	1	3

25. Read the following statements and choose the correct option(s) given below.

I. A seismic zone is an area which has high risk of earthquakes.

II. The point below the Earth's surface where earthquakes occur is known as epicentre.

Codes

(a) Only I
(b) Only II
(c) Both I and II
(d) None of these

Darken your choice with HB Pencil

1.	a b c d	6.	a b c d	11.	a b c d	16.	a b c d	21.	a b c d
2.	a b c d	7.	a b c d	12.	a b c d	17.	a b c d	22.	a b c d
3.	a b c d	8.	a b c d	13.	a b c d	18.	a b c d	23.	a b c d
4.	a b c d	9.	a b c d	14.	a b c d	19.	a b c d	24.	a b c d
5.	a b c d	10.	a b c d	15.	a b c d	20.	a b c d	25.	a b c d

03

Weather and Climate

MCQs 1 Mark Questions

1. .... is the condition of the atmosphere at a particular place and time.
   (a) Climate (b) Season
   (c) Weather (d) Monsoon

2. What is the average weather condition of a place over a long period of time called?
   (a) Atmosphere (b) Season
   (c) Climate (d) Weather

3. Identify the level of temperature of a place close to the equator.
   (a) Higher (b) Medium
   (c) Lower (d) Average

4. Complete the given analogy.
   Weather : ? : : Climate : Climatologists
   (a) Meteorologists (b) Scientists
   (c) Physicists (d) Doctor

5. Which of the following factor(s) affects the climate of a region?
   (a) Latitude (b) Altitude
   (c) Relief (d) All of these

6. Why does Shimla experiences a cooler climate than Delhi?
   (a) Shimla is situated at high altitude. (b) Delhi is situated at high altitude.
   (c) Delhi is far away from the sea. (d) None of these

7. During which months, the South-West Monsoon winds blow and bring rain to most of India?
   (a) June to September (b) October to January
   (c) March to June (d) August to December

8. The wind that blows from the sea to the land is called as ....
   (a) sea breeze (b) offshore wind
   (c) monsoon wind (d) land breeze

9. During what time in a day the sea breeze loses its heat slowly as compared to sea?
   (a) Morning (b) Afternoon
   (c) Night (d) Just after sunset

10. Why is/are Chennai said to be more humid than Jaisalmer?
    (a) Due to the differences in height above sea level.
    (b) Due to the difference in distance from the sea.
    (c) Both (a) and (b)
    (d) None of the above

11. .... is/are recognised as the largest geographical zones of the Earth.
    (a) Torrid zone (b) Frigid zone
    (c) Temperate zone (d) Both (b) and (c)

12. Which type of the climate is experiences by Torrid zone?
    (a) Wet climate (b) Tropical climate
    (c) Dry climate (d) None of these

13. Identify the zone which extends from the Tropic of Cancer to the Arctic circle in the Northern hemisphere and the Tropic of Capricorn to the Antarctic circle in the Southern hemisphere.
    (a) Temperate zone (b) Torrid zone
    (c) Frigid zone (d) None of these

14. Where is/are Frigid zone located?
    (a) Between the Arctic circle and North pole
    (b) Between the Arctic circle and South pole
    (c) Between North pole and South pole
    (d) Both (a) and (b)

15. Identify the country which does not falls under the Temperate zone?
    (a) USA (b) Russia
    (c) Malaysia (d) Germany

16. The habitat given in the picture below is an Igloo. Identify the region in which it is found.

(a) Polar region (b) Tropical region
(c) Continental region (d) Dry region

17. The Sun rays fall in a slant direction on which part of the globe?

(a) Equator (b) Northern hemisphere
(c) Southern hemisphere (d) Polar areas

MCQs 2 Marks Questions

18. Match the following.

List I	List II
A. Torrid zone	1. Moderate climate
B. Temperate zone	2. Hot climate
C. Frigid zone	3. Cold climate

Codes

	A	B	C		A	B	C
(a)	1	2	3	(b)	2	1	3
(c)	3	2	1	(d)	1	3	2

19. Read the given statements and select which ones are true (T) and which ones are false (F).

I. The vegetation of a place depends on its climate.

III. The climate of a place is affected by its distance from the sea.

Codes

	I	II		I	II
(a)	T	T	(b)	F	F
(c)	T	F	(d)	F	T

20. Identify the incorrect statement(s) about Frigid zone.

    I. The area around the poles is known as the Frigid zone.

    II. This zone receives extremely stanting rays of the Sun.

    Codes

    (c) Only I (d) Only II

    (c) Both I and II (d) Neither I nor II

21. Identify the region from the information given below.

    These are popular for their scenic beauty and many hill stations. They enjoy cool temperature in summers. The temperature in this region decreases as altitude increase.

    (a) Plains (b) Middle Himalayas

    (c) Foothills of Himalayas (d) None of these

22. Read the following statements and choose the incorrect option(s) given below.

    I. Mawsynram (Meghalaya) is the wettest place on the Earth.

    II. Humidity also affects the climate of a place as it causes rainfall.

    Codes

    (a) Only I (b) Only II

    (c) Both I and II (d) None of these

23. Read the given statements and select which ones are true (T) and which ones are false (F).

    I. Places situated near the coastal areas have humid weather conditions.

    II. Places which are away from sea/oceans record higher temperatures.

    Codes

	I	II		I	II
(a)	T	F	(b)	F	T
(c)	T	T	(d)	F	F

Darken your choice with HB Pencil

1. ⓐ ⓑ ⓒ ⓓ	5. ⓐ ⓑ ⓒ ⓓ	9. ⓐ ⓑ ⓒ ⓓ	13. ⓐ ⓑ ⓒ ⓓ	17. ⓐ ⓑ ⓒ ⓓ	21. ⓐ ⓑ ⓒ ⓓ
2. ⓐ ⓑ ⓒ ⓓ	6. ⓐ ⓑ ⓒ ⓓ	10. ⓐ ⓑ ⓒ ⓓ	14. ⓐ ⓑ ⓒ ⓓ	18. ⓐ ⓑ ⓒ ⓓ	22. ⓐ ⓑ ⓒ ⓓ
3. ⓐ ⓑ ⓒ ⓓ	7. ⓐ ⓑ ⓒ ⓓ	11. ⓐ ⓑ ⓒ ⓓ	15. ⓐ ⓑ ⓒ ⓓ	19. ⓐ ⓑ ⓒ ⓓ	23. ⓐ ⓑ ⓒ ⓓ
4. ⓐ ⓑ ⓒ ⓓ	8. ⓐ ⓑ ⓒ ⓓ	12. ⓐ ⓑ ⓒ ⓓ	16. ⓐ ⓑ ⓒ ⓓ	20. ⓐ ⓑ ⓒ ⓓ	

04

Our Country

MCQs 1 Mark Questions

1. .... carried by water during flood and it forms a fertile deposit on valley floor.
   (a) Sand (b) Silt (c) Mineral (d) Rock

2. The Chota Nagpur plateau is rich in which mineral?
   (a) Coal (b) Iron ore (c) Bauxite (d) All of these

3. The Southernmost point of the Indian territory is ....
   (a) Cape of Good Hope (b) Kanyakumari
   (c) Indira point (d) Himsagar point

4. Identify an East flowing river in India from the given options.
   (a) Krishna (b) Narmada (c) Ganga (d) Brahmaputra

5. Name the rivers which formed the Sundarban delta.
   (a) Ganga and Brahmaputra (b) Yamuna and Ganga
   (c) Godavari and Krishna (d) Tapi and Mahanadi

6. Where the rivers Alaknanda and Bhagirathi meets to form Ganga?
   (a) Devprayag (b) Vishnuprayag
   (c) Rudraprayag (d) Karnaprayag

7. The State of Uttar Pradesh shares its boundary with how many states?
   (a) 10 (b) 9 (c) 8 (d) 7

8. Among the following Union Territories of India, which is the smallest in geographical area?
   (a) Chandigarh (b) Puducherry
   (c) Dadra and Nagar Haveli (d) Lakshadweep

9. Identify the state with longest coastline in India.

(a) Goa (b) Gujarat (c) Andhra Pradesh (d) Tamil Nadu

10. India shares its land boundaries with which countries in the East?

(a) China, Nepal and Bhutan (b) Bhutan and Afghanistan
(c) Myanmar and Bangladesh (d) Pakistan and Afghanistan

11. Name the state from the given options that does not share its borders with Bangladesh.

(a) West Bengal (b) Odisha (c) Meghalaya (d) Tripura

12. Complete the given analogy regarding size of Indian states in terms of their population.

Largest state : Uttar Pradesh : : Smallest state : ?

(a) Sikkim (b) Goa (c) Nagaland (d) Ladakh

13. Where are Ajanta Caves located ?

(a) Gujarat (b) Maharashtra (c) Uttar Pradesh (d) Himachal Pradesh

14. Based on the picture given below, identify the state in which the given monument is situated.

(a) Telangana (b) Karnataka (c) Kerala (d) Tamil Nadu

15. .... is known as the land of forests.

(a) Kerala (b) Odisha (c) Jharkhand (d) Karnataka

16. How many historical and archaeological sites in India are recognised by UNESCO?

(a) 20 (b) 30 (c) 40 (d) 50

17. Which strait lies between India and Sri Lanka?

(a) Palk Strait (b) Malacca Strait (c) Bering Strait (d) Sunda Strait

18. Complete the given analogy.

Tamil Nadu : Bharatnatyam : : ? : Kuchipudi

(a) Kerala (b) Andhra Pradesh (c) Maharashtra (d) Assam

19. Who among the following is an Indian music director and classical flautist from Prayagraj (Allahabad) in Uttar Pradesh?

(a) Hariprasad Chaurasia (b) Zakir Hussain
(c) Ravi Shankar (d) Bismillah Khan

20. Unscramble the given letters to find out the name of folk dance which associate with Kerala.

(a) KILAKATAH (b) THAKAK (c) CHIKPUDUI (d) None of these

MCQs 2 Marks Questions

21. Read the given passage and fill in the blanks with appropriate words.

The Brihadeshwara temple is dedicated to Lord Shiva. It is located in Thanjavur, ... (I) ..... . It was built by ..... (II)...... .

	I	II
(a)	Karnataka	Rajaraja I
(b)	Tamil Nadu	Rajaraja I
(c)	Kerala	Rajendra I
(d)	Andhra Pradesh	Harihar and Bukka

22. Identify the fort from the information given below.

It is a historic fort located in India. The fort was built by Mughal Emperor Shah Jahan. It was designated as UNESCO World Heritage site in 2007.

(a) Golkonda Fort (b) Agra Fort
(c) Red Fort (d) None of these

23. Identify the incorrectly matched pair.

(a) Golkonda Fort – Jaipur
(b) Howrah Bridge – Kolkata
(c) Gateway of India – Mumbai
(d) Lotus Temple – Delhi

24. Identify the incorrectly matched pair.

State		Capital
(a) Nagaland	–	Kohima
(b) Tripura	–	Agartala
(c) Andhra Pradesh	–	Amravati
(d) Mizoram	–	Shillong

25. Match the following.

List I (Monuments)	List II (Location)
A. Fatehpur Sikri	1. Agra
B. Golden Temple	2. Amritsar
C. Ellora Caves	3. Aurangabad
D. Vivekananda Rock Memorial	4. Kanyakumari

Codes

	A	B	C	D		A	B	C	D
(a)	1	2	3	4	(b)	4	3	2	1
(c)	2	4	1	3	(d)	3	1	4	2

26. Which of the following is incorrect about the Himalayan mountains?

I. Himalayas are home to many glaciers and rivers.

II. Himalayas are not rich in minerals and resources.

Codes

(a) Only I (b) Only II (c) Both I and II (d) Neither I nor II

27. Read the given statements and select which ones are true (T) and which ones are false (F).

I. Sand Dunes are wind driven small hills of sand found in the desert.

II. Majuli is the world's largest river island, located in Assam.

Codes

	I	II		I	II		I	II		I	II
(a)	F	F	(b)	F	T	(c)	T	F	(d)	T	T

Darken your choice with HB Pencil

1.	a b c d	6.	a b c d	11.	a b c d	16.	a b c d	21.	a b c d	26.	a b c d
2.	a b c d	7.	a b c d	12.	a b c d	17.	a b c d	22.	a b c d	27.	a b c d
3.	a b c d	8.	a b c d	13.	a b c d	18.	a b c d	23.	a b c d		
4.	a b c d	9.	a b c d	14.	a b c d	19.	a b c d	24.	a b c d		
5.	a b c d	10.	a b c d	15.	a b c d	20.	a b c d	25.	a b c d		

05

Indian Freedom Struggle

MCQs 1 Mark Questions

1. **Who was the first Governor-General of Bengal?**
   (a) Robert Clive (b) Lord Cornwallis
   (c) Warren Hastings (d) William Bentinct

2. **................. was the first Governor-General of India.**
   (a) William Bentinck (b) Lord Dalhousie
   (c) Lord Canning (d) Lord Hardinge

3. **Sirajuddaula was the Nawab of which region?**
   (a) Bengal (b) Bihar (c) Lucknow (d) Bhopal

4. **Identify the battle in which Mir Qasim, Sirajuddaula and Shah Alam II were defeated by Hector Munro?**
   (a) Battle of Plassey (b) Battle of Buxar
   (c) Battle of Khanwa (d) Third Anglo Mysore War

5. **Who among the following were the first to come India with the purpose of trade?**
   (a) British (b) Portuguese
   (c) Dutch (d) French

6. **In which of the following places, the Ryotwari system was introduced?**
   (a) Bengal and Bihar (b) Bombay and Madras
   (c) Odisha and Uttar Pradesh (d) Bombay and Bhopal

7. **The Revolt of 1857 was started by ....**
   (a) the sepoys (b) the zamindars
   (c) the peasants (d) Both (a) and (c)

8. **Who among the following was the leader of the Revolt of 1857 from Kanpur?**
   (a) Bahadur Shah Zafar (b) Nana Saheb
   (c) Begum Hazarat Mahal (d) Rani Laxmi Bai

9. Which among the following events is known as the First War of Independence?

(a) The Swadeshi Movement (b) Civil Disobedience Movement
(c) Revolt of 1857 (d) Khilafat Movement

10. When did the first census in India take place under Lord Mayo as Viceroy?

(a) 1871 (b) 1872 (c) 1873 (d) 1874

11. The Indian National Congress (INC) was formed by which of the following personalities?

(a) AO Hume (b) Mahatma Gandhi
(c) Jawaharlal Nehru (d) Motilal Nehru

12. What was/were boycotted during the Swadeshi Movement?

(a) Foreign cloth (b) Salt (c) Both (a) and (b) (d) None of these

13. Where did Mahatma Gandhi launch the Civil Disobedience in 1930?

(a) Sabarmati Ashram (b) Ahmedabad
(c) Porbandar (d) Dandi

14. Complete the given analogy.
All India Forward Block : Subhash Chandra Bose : : Khilafat Movement : ?

(a) Mohd. Jinnah (b) Ali Brothers
(c) Maulana Abul Kalam (d) Sayed Ahmed

15. Identify the movement in which the slogan 'Do or Die' was given by Mahatma Gandhi.

(a) Non-Cooperation Movement (b) Quit India Movement
(c) Khilafat Movement (d) Civil Disobedience Movement

16. In which year, the Indian Independence Act was passed by the British Parliament?

(a) 1945 (b) 1942 (c) 1947 (d) 1946

17. Who among the following organised the Ghadar Party?

(a) VD Savarkar (b) Rash Behari Bose
(c) Lala Har Dayal (d) Madan Lal Dhingra

18. Who among the following exposed the economic drainage from India to Britain?

(a) Extremists (b) Moderates (c) Both (a) and (b) (d) Neither (a) nor (b)

19. When did the Jallianwala Bagh Massacre take place?

(a) 1938 (b) 1919 (c) 1934 (d) 1929

20. **Identify the Indian revolutionary shown in the picture given below.**

(a) Mahatma Gandhi (b) Motilal Nehru
(c) Rash Behari Bose (d) Gopal Krishna Gokhale

21. **Identify the famous personality who gave the slogan "Swaraj is my birthright and I shall have it".**

(a) Bipin Chandra Pal (b) Bal Gangadhar Tilak
(d) Lala Lajpat Rai (d) WC Bannerjee

22. **Complete the given analogy.**

Subsidiary Alliance : Lord Wellesley : : Doctrine of Lapse : ?

(a) Lord Dalhousie (b) Lord Mayo
(c) Lord Minto (d) General O'Dyer

23. **Who is known as the 'Father of Modern India'?**

(a) Mahatma Gandhi (b) Raja Ram Mohan Roy
(c) Pt Jawaharlal Nehru (d) Dadabhai Naoroji

MCQs 2 Marks Questions

24. **Match the following.**

List I (Leaders)	List II (Slogans)
A. Subhash Chandra Bose	1. Jai Hind
B. Jawaharlal Nehru	2. Aaram Haram Hai
C. Lal Bahadur Shastri	3. Jai Jawan Jai Kisan
D. Bhagat Singh	4. Inquilab Zindabad

Codes

	A	B	C	D		A	B	C	D
(a)	1	2	3	4	(b)	4	3	2	1
(c)	2	4	1	3	(d)	3	1	4	2

25. **Read the given statements associated with Dandi Satyagraha and select the option which ones are true (T) and which ones are false (F).**

I. It is also called as Civil Disobedience Movement.

II. It was the movement initiated by Mahatma Gandhi against the salt tax imposed by the British government in India.

III. Gandhiji started this movement from Sabarmati Ashram on 12th March, 1930.

Codes

	I	II		I	II
(a)	T	F	(b)	F	T
(c)	F	F	(d)	T	T

26. **Consider the following statements about extremist leaders and select the correct option.**

I. The goal of extremist leaders was 'Swaraj'.

II. They did not stick to constitutional methods to protest and demand.

Codes

(a) Only I (b) Only II (c) Both I and II (d) Neither I nor II

27. **Identify the personality from the information given below.**

- He was born into a Sikh family in 1907 in Lyallpur District, present-day Pakistan.
- He established the Hindustan Socialist Republican Association (HSRA) along with revolutionaries.

(a) Bhagat Singh (b) Sardar Udham Singh

(c) Prem Singh Dhillon (d) Sohan Singh Bhakna

Darken your choice with HB Pencil

1.	ⓐ ⓑ ⓒ ⓓ	6.	ⓐ ⓑ ⓒ ⓓ	11.	ⓐ ⓑ ⓒ ⓓ	16.	ⓐ ⓑ ⓒ ⓓ	21.	ⓐ ⓑ ⓒ ⓓ	26.	ⓐ ⓑ ⓒ ⓓ
2.	ⓐ ⓑ ⓒ ⓓ	7.	ⓐ ⓑ ⓒ ⓓ	12.	ⓐ ⓑ ⓒ ⓓ	17.	ⓐ ⓑ ⓒ ⓓ	22.	ⓐ ⓑ ⓒ ⓓ	27.	ⓐ ⓑ ⓒ ⓓ
3.	ⓐ ⓑ ⓒ ⓓ	8.	ⓐ ⓑ ⓒ ⓓ	13.	ⓐ ⓑ ⓒ ⓓ	18.	ⓐ ⓑ ⓒ ⓓ	23.	ⓐ ⓑ ⓒ ⓓ		
4.	ⓐ ⓑ ⓒ ⓓ	9.	ⓐ ⓑ ⓒ ⓓ	14.	ⓐ ⓑ ⓒ ⓓ	19.	ⓐ ⓑ ⓒ ⓓ	24.	ⓐ ⓑ ⓒ ⓓ		
5.	ⓐ ⓑ ⓒ ⓓ	10.	ⓐ ⓑ ⓒ ⓓ	15.	ⓐ ⓑ ⓒ ⓓ	20.	ⓐ ⓑ ⓒ ⓓ	25.	ⓐ ⓑ ⓒ ⓓ		

06

The Great Personalities

MCQs 1 Mark Questions

1. **Who among the following was a famous surgeon during 6th Century BC?**
(a) Kalidasa (b) Sushruta
(c) Panini (d) Bimbisara

2. **Identify the personality who is considered as the author of classical Indian medicine and Ayurveda.**
(a) Charaka (b) Brihat (c) Sushruta (d) Jivaka

3. **............. is regarded as India's greatest dramatist and poet.**
(a) Tulsidasa (b) Kalidasa (c) Meerabai (d) Amir Khusrau

4. **Which among the following is not written by Kalidasa?**
(a) Meghdootam (b) Ritusamhara
(c) Kumar Sambhav (d) Mricchakatikam

5. **Name the poet who won the Nobel Prize in 1913 in Literature.**
(a) Mahadevi Verma (b) Sri Aurobindo
(c) Rabindranath Tagore (d) Sumitranadan Pant

6. **Which among the following musicians was honoured with Bharat Ratna?**
(a) MS Subbhulakshmi (b) AR Rahman
(c) Hari Prasad Chaurasia (d) Illaiyaraja

7. **Who among the following was a prominent figure of Hindustani Classical Music?**
(a) Rahim (b) Tansen
(c) Chaitanya Mahaprabhu (d) Surdas

8. **Name the Indian freedom fighter who hoisted the Indian National Flag in Bombay during the Quit India Movement.**
(a) Aruna Asif Ali (b) Jawaharlal Nehru
(c) Khan Abdul Ghaffar Khan (d) Sucheta Kripalani

9. **Who was the founder of 'Shantiniketan'?**

(a) Mahatma Gandhi (b) Rabindranath Tagore
(c) Swami Vivekananda (d) Sri Aurobindo

10. **Identify the famous personality shown in the picture given below.**

(a) Savitri Bai Phule (b) Annie Besant
(c) Queen Victoria (d) Bhikaji Cama

11. **Teacher's Day is celebrated every year on 5th September in the honour of ....**

(a) S Radhakrishnan (b) Rajendra Prasad
(c) BR Ambedkar (d) Mahatma Gandhi

12. **The Aligarh Muslim University was founded by whom?**

(a) Syed Ahmed Khan (b) Muhammad Ali Jinnah
(c) Jawaharlal Nehru (d) Aruna Asaf Ali

13. **Complete the given analogy.**

Ram Krishna Mission : Swami Vivekananda : : Satyashodhak Samaj : ?

(a) Jyotiba Phule
(b) BR Ambedkar
(c) Sri Narayan Guru
(d) Raja Ram Mohan Roy

14. **Who among the following said "Go back to Vedas"?**

(a) Swami Vivekananda
(b) Swami Dayananda Saraswati
(c) Ram Krishna Paramhansa
(d) Rabindranath Tagore

15. Identify the personality shown in the picture given below.

(a) Bal Gangadhar Tilak
(b) Motilal Nehru
(c) Rajendra Lahiri
(d) Lala Lajpat Rai

16. Who among the following worked on educational reforms for women?

(a) Tarabai Shinde
(b) Dr Rukmabai
(c) Pandita Ramabai
(d) Bhikaiji Cama

17. What was the chief aim of the Brahmo Samaj?

(a) Promote education and social rights
(b) Worship of the eternal God
(c) Both (a) and (b)
(d) Improve the social conditions of Indian people

MCQs 2 Marks Questions

18. Identify the Indian revolutionary from the information given below.

He was a famous revolutionary. He gave the slogan 'Delhi Chalo'. He founded the 'Forward Block'. His jayanti is celebrated as 'Parakram Diwas'.

(a) Roshan Singh
(b) Subhash Chandra Bose
(c) VD Savarkar
(d) Mohan Singh

19. Match the following.

List I	List II
A. Sarojini Naidu	1. First woman Prime Minister of India
B. Annie Besant	2. First woman President of Indian National Congress
C. Indira Gandhi	3. First woman Social Reformer and Educationist
D. Savitri Bai Phule	4. Member of the Theosophical Society

Codes

	A	B	C	D		A	B	C	D
(a)	1	2	3	4	(b)	4	3	2	1
(c)	2	4	1	3	(d)	3	1	4	2

20. **Read the following statements and select which ones are true (T) and which ones are false (F).**

I. Tulsidasa was the author of Abhigyan Shakuntalam.

II. The National Anthem of India 'Jana Gana Mana' was written by Rabindranath Tagore.

Codes

	I	II		I	II		I	II		I	II
(a)	F	F	(b)	T	F	(c)	T	T	(d)	F	T

21. **Identify the personality from the information given below.**

He was born in Kolkata. He is regarded as the greatest poet of India. He did not believe in classroom education.

(a) Mahatma Gandhi (b) Swami Vivekananda
(c) Rabindranath Tagore (d) Sri Aurobindo

22. **Read the following statements and choose the correct code from options given below.**

I. Sucheta Kripalani was the first woman Chief Minister of India.

II. Indira Gandhi was named 'Woman of the Millennium' by BBC.

Codes

(a) Only I (b) Only II (c) Both I and II (d) Neither I nor II

23. **Which of the following was/were incorrect about Madan Mohan Malviya?**

I. He was born in Varanasi.

II. He founded the Benaras Hindu University.

Codes

(a) Only I (b) Only II (c) Both I and II (d) Neither I nor II

24. **Identify the incorrectly matched pair.**

	King		Poet
(a)	Harshavardhana	—	Banabhatta
(b)	Samudragupta	—	Harisena
(c)	Prithviraj Chauhan	—	Chand Bardai
(d)	Babur	—	Birbal

Darken your choice with HB Pencil

1. ⓐ ⓑ ⓒ ⓓ	5. ⓐ ⓑ ⓒ ⓓ	9. ⓐ ⓑ ⓒ ⓓ	13. ⓐ ⓑ ⓒ ⓓ	17. ⓐ ⓑ ⓒ ⓓ	21. ⓐ ⓑ ⓒ ⓓ
2. ⓐ ⓑ ⓒ ⓓ	6. ⓐ ⓑ ⓒ ⓓ	10. ⓐ ⓑ ⓒ ⓓ	14. ⓐ ⓑ ⓒ ⓓ	18. ⓐ ⓑ ⓒ ⓓ	22. ⓐ ⓑ ⓒ ⓓ
3. ⓐ ⓑ ⓒ ⓓ	7. ⓐ ⓑ ⓒ ⓓ	11. ⓐ ⓑ ⓒ ⓓ	15. ⓐ ⓑ ⓒ ⓓ	19. ⓐ ⓑ ⓒ ⓓ	23. ⓐ ⓑ ⓒ ⓓ
4. ⓐ ⓑ ⓒ ⓓ	8. ⓐ ⓑ ⓒ ⓓ	12. ⓐ ⓑ ⓒ ⓓ	16. ⓐ ⓑ ⓒ ⓓ	20. ⓐ ⓑ ⓒ ⓓ	24. ⓐ ⓑ ⓒ ⓓ

07

The Indian Government

MCQs 1 Mark Questions

1. **Which type of government system does India follow?**

(a) Presidential System
(b) Monarchy System
(c) Dictatorship
(d) Parliamentary System

2. **............. means people have the right to choose their own government.**

(a) Secular
(b) Democratic
(c) Socialist
(d) Justice

3. **How many levels of government does India have?**

(a) Three
(b) Two
(c) Four
(d) None of these

4. **Identify the system of government in which power is divided between a central authority and various constituent units of the country.**

(a) Monarchy
(b) Democracy
(c) Federalism
(d) None of these

5. **What is/are the feature(s) of Federal government?**

(a) Distribution of powers
(b) Rigidity
(c) Written Constitution
(d) All of these

6. **Complete the given analogy with regard to appointments.**

Chief Minister : Appointed by Governor :: Governor : ?

(a) Appointed by Chief Justice of Supreme Court
(b) Appointed by President
(c) Appointed by Prime Minister
(d) Appointed by Parliament

7. The maximum strength of Lok Sabha is ....

(a) 530 (b) 540 (c) 552 (d) 560

8. How many members of the Rajya Sabha are nominated by the President?

(a) 15 (b) 10 (c) 12 (d) 14

9. Who elects the Speaker of the House?

(a) The Prime Minister (b) The President
(c) Lok Sabha Members (d) Chief Justice of India

10. What is an eligibility criteria to become a member of Parliament?

(a) She/He should be above the age of 21.
(b) She/He should be a citizen of India.
(c) Both (a) and (b)
(d) None of the above

11. Complete the given analogy.

Lok Sabha : 5 years : : Rajya Sabha : ?

(a) 4 years (b) 6 years (c) 7 years (d) 5 years

12. Who among the following is the Commander in Chief of the armed forces?

(a) Governor (b) President
(c) Chief Minister (d) Prime Minister

13. Which is the highest court of Justice in India?

(a) Supreme Court (b) High Court
(c) Subordinate Court (d) All of these

14. Who is called as the 'Father of Indian Constitution'?

(a) BR Ambedkar (b) Rajendra Prasad
(c) Mahatma Gandhi (d) Jawaharlal Nehru

15. 26th January, 1950 is famous for which of the following events?

(a) Constitution of India was adopted (b) Constitution of India came into effect
(c) Draft Constitution passed (d) None of these

16. Which among the following is not a Fundamental Right?

(a) Right of Equality (b) Right to Freedom
(c) Cultural and Educational Rights (d) Right to Property

17. **How many Fundamental Duties are mentioned in Indian Constitution?**

(a) Ten (b) Eleven (c) Twelve (d) Nine

18. **Identify the monument in the picture given below from the following options.**

(a) Rashtrapati Bhavan (b) Jallianwala Bagh Memorial
(c) National War Memorial (d) None of these

MCQs 2 Marks Questions

19. **Read the following statements and choose the correct option(s) given below.**

I. The Government at the Centre is called the Union Government.

II. The Election Commission is headed by the Chief Election Commissioner.

Codes

(a) Only I (b) Only II (c) Both I and II (d) Neither I nor II

20. **Read the given statements and select which ones are true (T) and which ones are false (F).**

I. Only Indian citizens of 25 years of age and above can became members of the Lok Sabha.

II. The states are divided into smaller areas called Constituencies.

Codes

	I	II		I	II
(a)	T	F	(b)	F	F
(c)	T	T	(d)	F	T

21. **Which among the following is/are the Fundamental Duties?**

I. Uphold and protect the sovereignty and unity of India.

II. Safeguard public property and abjure violence.

Codes

(a) Only I (b) Only II (c) Both I and II (d) Neither I nor II

22. Match the following.

List I (Acts)	List II (Rights)
A. Right to Equality	1. Abolition of Untouchability
B. Right to Freedom	2. Right to Life and Personal Liberty
C. Cultural and Educational Rights	3. Protection of Language and Culture of Minorities
D. Right against Exploitation	4. Prohibition of Employment of Children in Hazardous Jobs

Codes

	A	B	C	D		A	B	C	D
(a)	1	2	3	4	(b)	4	3	2	1
(c)	3	1	4	2	(d)	2	4	1	3

23. Which of the following is/are correct about State Government?

I. State has a Upper House called Legislative Assembly or Vidhan Sabha.

II. Some Indian States have a Lower House called Legislative Council or Vidhan Parishad.

Codes

(a) Only I (b) Only II

(c) Both I and II (d) Neither I nor II

Darken your choice with HB Pencil

1. ⓐ ⓑ ⓒ ⓓ	5. ⓐ ⓑ ⓒ ⓓ	9. ⓐ ⓑ ⓒ ⓓ	13. ⓐ ⓑ ⓒ ⓓ	17. ⓐ ⓑ ⓒ ⓓ	21. ⓐ ⓑ ⓒ ⓓ
2. ⓐ ⓑ ⓒ ⓓ	6. ⓐ ⓑ ⓒ ⓓ	10. ⓐ ⓑ ⓒ ⓓ	14. ⓐ ⓑ ⓒ ⓓ	18. ⓐ ⓑ ⓒ ⓓ	22. ⓐ ⓑ ⓒ ⓓ
3. ⓐ ⓑ ⓒ ⓓ	7. ⓐ ⓑ ⓒ ⓓ	11. ⓐ ⓑ ⓒ ⓓ	15. ⓐ ⓑ ⓒ ⓓ	19. ⓐ ⓑ ⓒ ⓓ	23. ⓐ ⓑ ⓒ ⓓ
4. ⓐ ⓑ ⓒ ⓓ	8. ⓐ ⓑ ⓒ ⓓ	12. ⓐ ⓑ ⓒ ⓓ	16. ⓐ ⓑ ⓒ ⓓ	20. ⓐ ⓑ ⓒ ⓓ	

08

The United Nations

MCQs 1 Mark Questions

1. **In which year United Nations was established?**

(a) 1932 (b) 1939 (c) 1945 (d) 1950

2. **The United Nations Day is celebrated on .... every year.**

(a) 24th October (b) 30th April (c) 5th January (d) 16th November

3. **Who prepares reports, keeps records and carries out the day to day activities of the UN?**

(a) General Assembly (b) Security Council
(c) Secretariat (d) International Court of Justice

4. **Which among the following is/are the organs of the UNs?**

(a) General Assembly (b) Security Council
(c) Secretariat (d) All of these

5. **Who among the following gave United Nations its name?**

(a) Abraham Lincoln (b) Franklin D Roosevelt
(c) George Washington (d) None of these

6. **Identify the organ which is responsible for maintaining international peace and security in the world.**

(a) General Assembly (b) Secretariat
(c) Security Council (d) Economic and Social Council

7. **Which among the following is/are the permanent members of the Security Council?**

(a) France (b) Russia (c) China (d) All of these

8. **Complete the given analogy.**
General Assembly : ? : : Economic and Social Council : 54 members

(a) 192 members (b) 194 members (c) 193 members (d) 190 members

9. **The International Court of Justice is located in which of the following countries?**

(a) America (b) Netherlands (c) Russia (d) Germany

10. How many judges are there in International Court?
(a) 10 (b) 15 (c) 20 (d) 25

11. Which among the followings is/are the agencies of the United Nations?
(a) UNESCO (b) ILO (c) UNICEF (d) All of these

12. Identify the agency of the UN whose flag is shown in the picture given below.

(a) UNICEF (b) WHO (c) FAO (d) ILO

13. .... works to improve the health and welfare of the people around the world.
(a) FAO (b) Security Council (c) WHO (d) UNESCO

14. Complete the given analogy.
WHO : Switzerland : : FAO : ?
(a) Italy (b) France (c) England (d) China

15. When did India join the UN ?
(a) 1945 (b) 1950 (c) 1957 (d) 1975

16. Identify the women who was elected as the first woman President of the UN General Assembly.

(a)  (b)  (c)  (d) 

17. In which country, India has sent its peace keeping forces as part of UN mission?
(a) Congo (b) Sudan
(c) Both (a) and (b) (d) None of these

MCQs 2 Marks Questions

18. Read the given information and answer the following question.
I am the agency of UN. My aim is solving problems related to food and agriculture.
Who am I?
(a) UNICEF (b) WHO (c) FAO (d) ILO

19. **Which among the following statements is/are incorrect?**

I. The United Nations was established after the Second World War.

II. The headquarters of the two UNs body is located in New York.

Codes

(a) Only I (b) Only II (c) Both I and II (d) None of these

20. **Match the following.**

	List I (Organisation)		List II (Headquarters)
A.	United Nations	1.	Rome
B.	WHO	2.	Paris
C.	UNESCO	3.	Geneva
D.	FAO	4.	New York

Codes

	A	B	C	D		A	B	C	D
(a)	4	3	2	1	(b)	1	2	3	4
(c)	2	4	1	3	(d)	3	1	4	2

21. **Read the given statements and select which ones are true (T) and which ones are false (F).**

I. UNICEF works for child rights around the world.

II. UNESCO works towards the educational, scientific and cultural development of the world.

Codes

	I	II		I	II		I	II		I	II
(a)	T	F	(b)	F	T	(c)	T	T	(d)	F	F

22. **Identify the organ of the UN from the information given below.**

It helps to resolve the Economic and Social issues of the world. It aims to improving the living conditions of the people all over the world. It protects Human Rights.

(a) International Court of Justice (b) Economic and Social Council

(c) Secretariat (d) General Assembly

Darken your choice with HB Pencil

1.	ⓐ ⓑ ⓒ ⓓ	5.	ⓐ ⓑ ⓒ ⓓ	9.	ⓐ ⓑ ⓒ ⓓ	13.	ⓐ ⓑ ⓒ ⓓ	17.	ⓐ ⓑ ⓒ ⓓ	21.	ⓐ ⓑ ⓒ ⓓ
2.	ⓐ ⓑ ⓒ ⓓ	6.	ⓐ ⓑ ⓒ ⓓ	10.	ⓐ ⓑ ⓒ ⓓ	14.	ⓐ ⓑ ⓒ ⓓ	18.	ⓐ ⓑ ⓒ ⓓ	22.	ⓐ ⓑ ⓒ ⓓ
3.	ⓐ ⓑ ⓒ ⓓ	7.	ⓐ ⓑ ⓒ ⓓ	11.	ⓐ ⓑ ⓒ ⓓ	15.	ⓐ ⓑ ⓒ ⓓ	19.	ⓐ ⓑ ⓒ ⓓ		
4.	ⓐ ⓑ ⓒ ⓓ	8.	ⓐ ⓑ ⓒ ⓓ	12.	ⓐ ⓑ ⓒ ⓓ	16.	ⓐ ⓑ ⓒ ⓓ	20.	ⓐ ⓑ ⓒ ⓓ		

09

Agriculture and Industries

MCQs 1 Mark Questions

1. **Which sector is the backbone of Indian Economy?**
   (a) Service sector (b) Financial sector
   (c) Tourism sector (d) Agriculture sector

2. **'Slash and burn' agriculture is a type of ....**
   (a) shifting agriculture (b) intensive agriculture
   (c) commercial agriculture (d) subsistence farming

3. **During which months, Rabi crops are harvested?**
   (a) June to August (b) April to June
   (c) April to May (d) May to July

4. **Rice is a Kharif crop that requires annual rainfall above ....**
   (a) 200 cm (b) 50 cm
   (c) 100 cm (d) 250 cm

5. **Which among the following is/are the Commercial crops of India?**
   (a) Mustard (b) Tobacco
   (c) Jute (d) All of these

6. **Identify the Indian state which is the largest producer of coffee.**
   (a) Tamil Nadu (b) Assam
   (c) Karnataka (d) Kerala

7. **Which one of the following is a Cash crop?**
   (a) Wheat (b) Millets
   (c) Rice (d) Rubber

8. **Identify the Kharif crop from the options given below.**

(a)

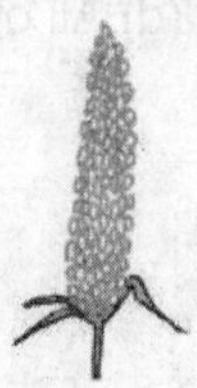

(b)

(c)

(d)

9. **Blue Revolution is associated with which of the following?**
(a) Fruits production (b) Fish production
(c) Egg production (d) Milk production

10. **Complete the analogy about largest producers.**
Gujarat : Soybean : : Wheat : ?
(a) Punjab (b) Uttar Pradesh (c) West Bengal (d) Assam

11. **Livestock rearing is also called as ....**
(a) Sericulture (b) Viticulture (c) Animal Husbandry (d) None of these

12. **Name the type of industry which can be set-up by the people in their homes.**
(a) Shipping industry (b) Cottage industry
(c) Automobile industry (d) Textile industry

13. **Identify the type of industry which is shown in the picture given below.**

(a) Cottage industry (b) Automobile industry
(c) Heavy industry (d) None of these

14. **Which of the following is not an agro-based industry?**
(a) Vegetable oil industry (b) Cotton textile industry
(c) Leather industry (d) Fish oil manufacturing industry

15. Identify the requirements of a large-scale industry from the following.
(a) Raw materials (b) Money (c) Manpower (d) All of these

16. Complete the given analogy.
Electronic industry : Computer : : ? : Car
(a) Automobile industry (b) Aviation industry
(c) Textile industry (d) Shipping industry

17. Where is the largest shipbuilding unit on the Western Coast of India located?
(a) Goa (b) Mumbai (c) Kochi (d) Surat

18. What is/are the advantage(s) of tourism industry?
(a) It preserve the natural environment. (b) It promotes international connection.
(c) It provides jobs and career. (d) All of these

19. Which among the following is/are the example(s) of Heavy Industry?
(a) Aircraft industry (b) Railway equipment industry
(c) Shipbuilding industry (d) All of these

MCQs 2 Marks Questions

20. Identify the industry from the information given below.
This industry needs huge capital. It provides large number of employment.
(a) Cottage industry (b) Heavy industry
(c) Paper bag industry (d) None of these

21. Which of the following is/are a Kharif crop?
I. Jawar II. Maize III. Groundnut IV. Wheat
Codes
(a) Only I (b) Both I and II (c) I, II and III (d) All of these

22. Read the given statements and select which ones are true (T) and which ones are false (F).
I. Tata Iron and Steel Company is located in Jamshedpur, Jharkhand.
II. Khetri, Rajasthan is famous for copper mines.

Codes

	I	II		I	II
(a)	T	F	(b)	T	T
(c)	F	T	(d)	F	F

23. **Match the following.**

	List I (City)	List II (Famous for)
A.	Jalandhar	1. Sports Industry
B.	Kanchipuram	2. Silk saree Industry
C.	Surat	3. Textile Industry
D.	Moradabad	4. Brass work Industry

Codes

	A	B	C	D		A	B	C	D
(a)	1	2	3	4	(b)	4	3	2	1
(c)	2	1	4	3	(d)	3	4	1	2

24. **Identify the correctly matched pair.**

(a) Silicon Valley of India – Chennai
(b) Steel city of India – Bhilai
(c) Manchester of India – Ahmedabad
(d) Milk city – Porbandar

25. **On the given map of India, a city is marked as A. It is famous industrial city of Odisha. Identify the city.**

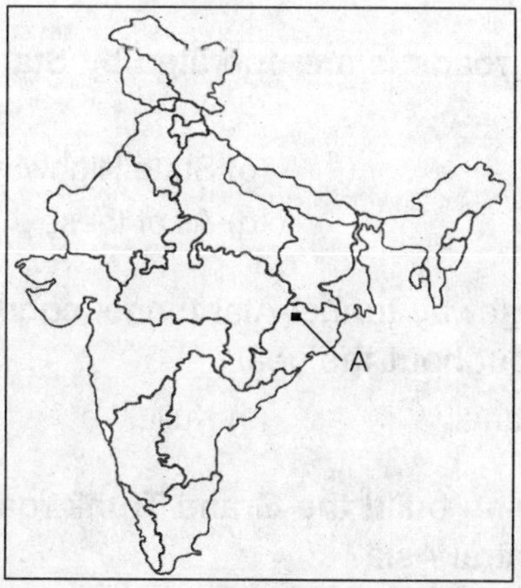

(a) Mumbai (b) Kolkata (c) Gangtok (d) Rourkela

Darken your choice with HB Pencil

1.	ⓐ ⓑ ⓒ ⓓ	6.	ⓐ ⓑ ⓒ ⓓ	11.	ⓐ ⓑ ⓒ ⓓ	16.	ⓐ ⓑ ⓒ ⓓ	21.	ⓐ ⓑ ⓒ ⓓ
2.	ⓐ ⓑ ⓒ ⓓ	7.	ⓐ ⓑ ⓒ ⓓ	12.	ⓐ ⓑ ⓒ ⓓ	17.	ⓐ ⓑ ⓒ ⓓ	22.	ⓐ ⓑ ⓒ ⓓ
3.	ⓐ ⓑ ⓒ ⓓ	8.	ⓐ ⓑ ⓒ ⓓ	13.	ⓐ ⓑ ⓒ ⓓ	18.	ⓐ ⓑ ⓒ ⓓ	23.	ⓐ ⓑ ⓒ ⓓ
4.	ⓐ ⓑ ⓒ ⓓ	9.	ⓐ ⓑ ⓒ ⓓ	14.	ⓐ ⓑ ⓒ ⓓ	19.	ⓐ ⓑ ⓒ ⓓ	24.	ⓐ ⓑ ⓒ ⓓ
5.	ⓐ ⓑ ⓒ ⓓ	10.	ⓐ ⓑ ⓒ ⓓ	15.	ⓐ ⓑ ⓒ ⓓ	20.	ⓐ ⓑ ⓒ ⓓ	25.	ⓐ ⓑ ⓒ ⓓ

10

Transport and Communication

MCQs 1 Mark Questions

1. India has second largest .... network in the world.
(a) roadways (b) railways (c) waterways (d) over all transport

2. Identify the longest National Highway of India from the following options.
(a) NH-44 (b) NH-27 (c) NH-6 (d) NH-34

3. The National Highway (NH-1) is the oldest NH of India. It connects .... to Amritsar.
(a) Lucknow (b) Delhi (c) Agra (d) Jalandhar

4. Which of the following roads is/are operated by State Public Works Department (PWD)?
(a) National Highways (b) State Highways
(c) District Roads (d) All of these

5. The world's longest highway tunnel-Atal tunnel connects which city to Lahaul-Spiti Valley throughout the year?
(a) Shimla (b) Manali (c) Kullu (d) Dharamshala

6. Who among the following build the Grand Trunk road which connects the Indian sub-continent with Central Asia?
(a) Sher Shah Suri (b) Genghis Khan
(c) Humayun (d) Babur

7. Complete the given analogy with regards to the Grand Trunk road.
India : Kolkata :: Pakistan : ?
(a) Islamabad (b) Lahore (c) Peshawar (d) Karachi

8. When was the first railway run in India?
(a) 1833 (b) 1853 (c) 1943 (d) 1973

9. **Into how many zones Indian Railways is divided?**
(a) 16 (b) 19 (c) 17 (d) 22

10. **In which city the first Metro rail was introduced ?**
(a) Delhi (b) Mumbai (c) Bengaluru (d) Kolkata

11. **Identify the city in which the headquarters of Indian Railway is located.**
(a) Mumbai (b) Kolkata (c) New Delhi (d) Chennai

12. **Identify the National Waterways that connects Prayagraj (Allahabad) to Haldia.**
(a) NW-1 (b) NW-2 (c) NW-3 (d) NW-4

13. **Which of the following rivers is/are used for transportation?**
(a) Hwang Ho river (b) Rhine river
(c) Brahmaputra river (d) All of these

14. **Mention the names of the seas that are joined by the Suez Canal.**
(a) The Mediterranean and Red Sea (b) Black and Mediterranean Sea
(c) The North Sea and Baltic Sea (d) The Baltic Sea and White Sea

15. **The longest Railway tunnel in the world i.e. the Gotthard Base is located in which country?**
(a) Switzerland (b) Germany (c) Russia (d) USA

16. **Who among the following is regarded as the 'Father of Long Distance Radio Transmission'?**
(a) Guglielmo Marconi (b) Graham Bell
(c) Wright Brothers (d) Samuel Morse

17. **Identify the means of transportation from the image given below.**

(a) Metro (b) Tram (c) Trains (d) Goods Train

18. Complete the given analogy.

Lal Bahadur Shastri Airport : ? : : Chhatrapati Shivaji Maharaj Airport : Mumbai

(a) Kochi
(b) Lucknow
(c) Bhubaneswar
(d) Varanasi

19. The Trans-Siberian Railway in .... is the longest rail route in the world with a length of 9,289 kms.

(a) Urals
(b) Europe
(c) Russia
(d) across Central Asia

20. Which of the following is the busiest sea-route in the world?

(a) North Atlantic Route
(b) Mediterranean Route
(c) Pacific Ocean
(d) South Atlantic Route

21. In 1903, the Wright Brothers flew the first airplane. What was its name?

(a) Sky flyer
(b) Birdie
(c) Flyer
(d) None of these

MCQs 2 Marks Questions

22. Match the following.

List I (Port)	List II (State)
A. Deendayal Port	1. Gujarat
B. Tuticorin Port	2. Tamil Nadu
C. Jawaharlal Nehru Port	3. Maharashtra
D. Mormugao Port	4. Goa

Codes

	A	B	C	D
(a)	1	2	3	4
(b)	4	3	2	1
(c)	3	1	4	2
(d)	2	4	1	3

23. Identify the incorrect statement(s) regarding Indian Railways.

I. The Indian Railways operates in three different gauges.

II. The Bharatmala Projects are associated with the railways.

Codes

(a) Only I
(b) Only II
(c) Both I and II
(d) None of these

24. **Look at the given pictures, which shows different types of means of communication and answer the question that follow.**

P

Q

R

S

I. Which among these was invented by Alexander Graham Bell?

II. Which of these was invented by G Marconi?

Codes

	I	II
(a)	P	Q
(b)	R	S
(c)	Q	R
(d)	P	S

25. **Read the given statements and select which ones are true (T) and which ones are false (F).**

I. Astronauts use rocket and spacecraft to travel in space.

II. JRD Tata was the first person to take a solo flight from Mumbai to Karachi.

Codes

	I	II		I	II
(a)	T	F	(b)	F	T
(c)	T	T	(d)	F	F

26. **Identify the personality from the information given below.**

They were American Brothers. They invented the first successful airplane. Both brothers attended high school but did not receive diploma.

(a) Orville Wright and Wilbur Wright (b) Wilbar Wright and Samuel Wright

(c) Samuel Wright and Orville Wright (d) None of these

Darken your choice with HB Pencil

1.	ⓐ ⓑ ⓒ ⓓ	6.	ⓐ ⓑ ⓒ ⓓ	11.	ⓐ ⓑ ⓒ ⓓ	16.	ⓐ ⓑ ⓒ ⓓ	21.	ⓐ ⓑ ⓒ ⓓ	26.	ⓐ ⓑ ⓒ ⓓ
2.	ⓐ ⓑ ⓒ ⓓ	7.	ⓐ ⓑ ⓒ ⓓ	12.	ⓐ ⓑ ⓒ ⓓ	17.	ⓐ ⓑ ⓒ ⓓ	22.	ⓐ ⓑ ⓒ ⓓ		
3.	ⓐ ⓑ ⓒ ⓓ	8.	ⓐ ⓑ ⓒ ⓓ	13.	ⓐ ⓑ ⓒ ⓓ	18.	ⓐ ⓑ ⓒ ⓓ	23.	ⓐ ⓑ ⓒ ⓓ		
4.	ⓐ ⓑ ⓒ ⓓ	9.	ⓐ ⓑ ⓒ ⓓ	14.	ⓐ ⓑ ⓒ ⓓ	19.	ⓐ ⓑ ⓒ ⓓ	24.	ⓐ ⓑ ⓒ ⓓ		
5.	ⓐ ⓑ ⓒ ⓓ	10.	ⓐ ⓑ ⓒ ⓓ	15.	ⓐ ⓑ ⓒ ⓓ	20.	ⓐ ⓑ ⓒ ⓓ	25.	ⓐ ⓑ ⓒ ⓓ		

11

Evolution of Mankind

MCQs 1 Mark Questions

1. **Who among the following was the first man that started burying their dead?**
   (a) Homo Erectus (b) Homo Sapiens
   (c) Cro-Magnon (d) None of these

2. **Which of the following is also known as the Lithic age?**
   (a) Stone age (b) Old stone age
   (c) Mesolithic age (d) Paleolithic age

3. **Identify the age which is also known as Middle stone age?**
   (a) Iron age (b) Mesolithic age
   (c) Neolithic age (d) Paleolithic age

4. **The earliest evidence of domesticating the animals have been found from ....**
   (a) Mehsana, Gujarat (b) Adamgarh, Madhya Pradesh
   (c) Pratapgarh, Uttar Pradesh (d) Rajgir, Bihar

5. **Name the first animal that was domesticated by early humans.**
   (a) horse (b) dog
   (c) cow (d) donkey

6. **The main cultivated crops of Neolithic men was/were ....**
   (a) wheat (b) barley
   (c) paddy (d) All of these

7. **Which of the following was the first metal used by Neolithic people?**
   (a) Iron (b) Bronze
   (c) Copper (d) Silver

8. **The oldest evidence of wheat and barley cultivation was found from which place?**
   (a) Banawali (b) Mehrgarh
   (c) Allahabad (Prayagraj) (d) Kalibangan

9. **In which age, the men started growing cotton and learn about clothes?**
(a) Neolithic age (b) Mesolithic age
(c) Paleolithic age (d) None of these

10. **Identify the period in which hand-made pottery and use of potter wheel first appeared.**
(a) Neolithic age (b) Chalcolithic age
(c) Middle stone age (d) Paleolithic stone age

11. **Complete the given analogy.**
Neolithic age : Use of polished stone tools : : ? : Copper was used
(a) Mesolithic age (b) Chalcolithic age
(c) Neolithic age (d) Megalithic age

12. **Select the correct Chalcolithic site from the following options.**
(a) Ahar (b) Jorwe
(c) Malwa and Rangpur (d) All of these

13. **Brahmagiri is related to which of the following sites?**
(a) Palaeolithic (b) Neolithic
(c) Megalithic (d) Mesolithic

14. **Complete the given analogy.**
BC : Before Christ : : AD : ?
(a) After Date (b) After Death (Christ's)
(c) Anna Domini (d) None of these

15. **The people of which of the following age were the first to use the painted pottery?**
(a) Chalcolithic age (b) Paleolithic age
(c) Mesolithic age (d) Neolithic age

16. **Rice was grown first in which of the following places?**
(a) North of Vindhyas (b) South of Vindhyas
(c) North of Narmada (d) South of Godavari

17. **Bhimbetka, an ancient Paleolithic site is situated in which state of modern India?**
(a) Madhya Pradesh (b) Jharkhand
(c) Bihar (d) Uttar Pradesh

18. **Early evidence of Neolithic culture is found in ....**

(a) Indus Valley Civilisation (b) Mesopotamian Civilisation
(c) Egyptian Civilisation (d) All of these

MCQs 2 Marks Questions

19. **Identify the period with the help of information given below.**

- **During this period, the ochre-coloured pottery was popular.**
- **People during this period lived in thatched houses made of mud and bricks.**

Codes

(a) Iron age (b) Stone age
(c) Chalcolithic age (d) Paleolithic

20. **Arrange the following in chronological order.**

I. Iron age
II. Copper age
III. Bronze age

Codes

(a) II, III, I (b) I, II, III
(c) III, II, I (d) II, I, III

21. **Read the given statements and select which ones are true (T) and which ones are false (F).**

I. The early Stone age sites have been found in the Valley of river Son or Sohan in Punjab (now, in Punjab).

II. The people of Mesolithic period believed in life after death.

Codes

	I	II
(a)	T	F
(b)	T	T
(c)	F	F
(d)	F	T

22. **Which among the following is/are correct about Neolithic age?**

(a) It is also refer to the last Stone age.
(b) People of Neolithic age used tools and weapon made of bone.
(c) They domesticated cattle, sheep and goats as well.
(d) All of the above

23. Among the following statements, choose the incorrect option regarding Paleolithic age.

(a) The life of these people was totally primitive.

(b) They were dependent on farming.

(c) Their food was not cooked.

(d) They had not certain dwelling place.

24. Match the following.

List I (Sites)	List II (Present Day States)
A. Burzahom	1. Jammu and Kashmir
B. Hallur	2. Karnataka
C. Mehrgarh	3. Pakistan

Codes

	A	B	C		A	B	C
(a)	1	2	3	(b)	3	2	1
(c)	2	1	3	(d)	1	3	2

25. Which among the following is/are true about Mesolithic age?

(a) They were aware of burial process of the dead bodies.

(b) They were dependent on hunting.

(c) They started domesticating animals like dog, sheep, goat, cow, ox and buffalo.

(d) All of the above

Darken your choice with HB Pencil

1.	ⓐ ⓑ ⓒ ⓓ	6.	ⓐ ⓑ ⓒ ⓓ	11.	ⓐ ⓑ ⓒ ⓓ	16.	ⓐ ⓑ ⓒ ⓓ	21.	ⓐ ⓑ ⓒ ⓓ
2.	ⓐ ⓑ ⓒ ⓓ	7.	ⓐ ⓑ ⓒ ⓓ	12.	ⓐ ⓑ ⓒ ⓓ	17.	ⓐ ⓑ ⓒ ⓓ	22.	ⓐ ⓑ ⓒ ⓓ
3.	ⓐ ⓑ ⓒ ⓓ	8.	ⓐ ⓑ ⓒ ⓓ	13.	ⓐ ⓑ ⓒ ⓓ	18.	ⓐ ⓑ ⓒ ⓓ	23.	ⓐ ⓑ ⓒ ⓓ
4.	ⓐ ⓑ ⓒ ⓓ	9.	ⓐ ⓑ ⓒ ⓓ	14.	ⓐ ⓑ ⓒ ⓓ	19.	ⓐ ⓑ ⓒ ⓓ	24.	ⓐ ⓑ ⓒ ⓓ
5.	ⓐ ⓑ ⓒ ⓓ	10.	ⓐ ⓑ ⓒ ⓓ	15.	ⓐ ⓑ ⓒ ⓓ	20.	ⓐ ⓑ ⓒ ⓓ	25.	ⓐ ⓑ ⓒ ⓓ

12

Inventions and Discoveries

MCQs 1 Mark Questions

1. .... were the first to use the alphabetic system of writing.
(a) Greeks (b) Sumerians (c) Europeans (d) China

2. Paper was first used in which of the following countries?
(a) America (b) China (c) India (d) Russia

3. The printing press was developed by Johannes Gutenberg in 1430 from which country he belonged to?
(a) France (b) Germany (c) America (d) China

4. For which of the following people, the Braille Script was invented by Louis Braille?
(a) Mentally disturbed (b) Visually impaired
(c) Verbally impaired (d) Physically challenged

5. Who among the following invented electricity?
(a) Benjamin Franklin (b) Daniel Fahrenheit
(c) Louis Pasteur (d) Edward Jenner

6. Complete the given analogy.
Steam Engine : ? : : Petrol Engine : Daimler
(a) Thomas Newcomen (b) Rudolf Diesel
(c) Benjamin Franklin (d) Edward Jenner

7. When was the Steam Engine invented?
(a) 1712 (b) 1769 (c) 1764 (d) 1780

8. What is the script in which Hindi is written?
(a) Devanagari (b) Dravidian (c) Hieroglyphic (d) None of these

9. **Identify the instrument which is used to measure body temperature.**

(a) Thermometer (b) Stethoscope
(c) MRI Machine (d) Both (a) and (b)

10. **............ is an instrument that enables us to see very small objects which cannot be seen through unaided eyes by enlarging their size.**

(a) MRI Machine (b) Microscope
(c) Telescope (d) Stethoscope

11. **What temperature is taken as normal body temperature?**

(a) 98.4° F (b) 37°F (c) 98.4°C (d) 99°F

12. **Who discovered the antibiotic called Penicillin?**

(a) Joseph Lister (b) Edward Jenner
(c) Alexander Fleming (d) Louis Pasteur

13. **Edward Jenner invented the first vaccine against which of the following diseases?**

(a) Small pox (b) Malaria (c) Cholera (d) Dengue fever

14. **What is the method of killing of germs called?**

(a) Distillation (b) Sterilisation
(c) Sublimation (d) Pasteurisation

15. **Who discovered that disease causing germs were present in water and milk?**

(a) Louis Pasteur (b) Daniel Fahrenheit
(c) Alexander Fleming (d) Joseph Lister

16. **The process of killing or removing harmful germs from a substance is called ....**

(a) Evaporation (b) Sterilisation
(c) Pasteurisation (d) Sublimation

17. **Complete the given analogy.**

Telescope : Hans Lippershey : Calculator : ?

(a) Galileo (b) James Watt
(c) Blaise Pascal (d) John Dalton

18. **Which medical device plots the heartbeats in the form of a graph ?**

(a) MRI (b) ECG (c) X-ray (d) USG

19. **Identify the medical device shown in the picture given below.**

(a) Ultrasound (b) X-ray (c) ECG (d) MRI Machine

MCQs 2 Marks Questions

20. **Identify the medical device from the information given below.**

- **Dr Rene Laennec invented this in 1816.**
- **It is used to listen the sounds of the internal organs of our body such as lungs and heart.**

(a) Microscope (b) Thermometer (c) Stethoscope (d) Laser

21. **Read the given statements and select which ones are true (T) and which ones are false (F).**

I. Antiseptic kills bacteria and helps to protect wounds from getting infected.
II. The process of giving someone vaccine is called vaccination.

Codes

	I	II
(a)	T	T
(b)	F	T
(c)	F	F
(d)	T	F

22. **Consider the following statements and select the correct option.**

I. Wheel was first invented by Egyptians.
II. India was the first to make use of paper currency.

Codes

(a) Only I (b) Only II (c) Both I and II (d) Neither I nor II

Darken your choice with HB Pencil

1.	ⓐ ⓑ ⓒ ⓓ	5.	ⓐ ⓑ ⓒ ⓓ	9.	ⓐ ⓑ ⓒ ⓓ	13.	ⓐ ⓑ ⓒ ⓓ	17.	ⓐ ⓑ ⓒ ⓓ	21.	ⓐ ⓑ ⓒ ⓓ
2.	ⓐ ⓑ ⓒ ⓓ	6.	ⓐ ⓑ ⓒ ⓓ	10.	ⓐ ⓑ ⓒ ⓓ	14.	ⓐ ⓑ ⓒ ⓓ	18.	ⓐ ⓑ ⓒ ⓓ	22.	ⓐ ⓑ ⓒ ⓓ
3.	ⓐ ⓑ ⓒ ⓓ	7.	ⓐ ⓑ ⓒ ⓓ	11.	ⓐ ⓑ ⓒ ⓓ	15.	ⓐ ⓑ ⓒ ⓓ	19.	ⓐ ⓑ ⓒ ⓓ		
4.	ⓐ ⓑ ⓒ ⓓ	8.	ⓐ ⓑ ⓒ ⓓ	12.	ⓐ ⓑ ⓒ ⓓ	16.	ⓐ ⓑ ⓒ ⓓ	20.	ⓐ ⓑ ⓒ ⓓ		

Practice Set 01

Time : 60 Mins. Max. Marks : 60

General Instructions

1. This question paper contains 50 questions.
2. All questions are compulsory. There is no negative marking.
3. This question paper is divided into two parts; In Part I, there are 40 MCQs of 1 mark each while in Part II, there are 10 MCQs of 2 marks each.
4. Use HB pencil / Blue ball point pen to mark your choice of answer by darkening the circles on the OMR Sheet.

MCQs 1 Mark Questions

1. Which of the following processes is being utilised while composting biodegradable waste

(a) Refusing
(b) Reducing
(c) Reusing
(d) Recycling

2. How the British took over control of India?

(a) By Subsidiary Alliance
(b) By Doctrine of Lapse
(c) By Divide and Rule Policy
(d) All of the above

3. Identify the zone(s) which receive the maximum heat from the Sun.

(a) Tropical Zone
(b) Frigid Zone
(c) Temperate Zone
(d) All of the above

4. Complete the given analogy.

Term of Lok Sabha Member : 5 years :: Term of Rajya Sabha Member : ?

(a) 4 years (b) 5 years
(c) 6 years (d) 7 years

5. The part of the Indian Constitution which expressly declares that India is a Sovereign, Socialist, Secular and Democratic Republic is/are .... .

(a) Fundamental Rights
(b) Directive Principles of State Policy
(c) Preamble
(d) Fundamental Duties

6. The personality given below is of Mangal Pandey. He is associated with which of the following historical event?

(a) First War of Independence
(b) Quit India Movement
(c) Battle of Buxar
(d) Khilafat Movement

7. .... is a cartographer.

(a) One that creates maps
(b) One that creates globes
(c) One that has created the map scales
(d) One that has created the map grids

8. What is the minimum age required to become a member of Lok Sabha?

(a) 21 years (b) 24 years
(c) 25 years (d) 30 years

9. On which day, UN day is celebrated every year?

(a) 24th September (b) 24th October
(c) 24th November (d) 24th December

10. Why plateaus are important for us?

(a) They are rich in mineral resources.
(b) They form a natural barrier against hot and cold winds.
(c) They are thickly populated.
(d) They are home to large variety of flora and fauna.

11. How many members are nominated by the President of India in Upper House of the Parliament?

(a) 10 members (b) 15 members
(c) 11 members (d) 12 members

12. Who among the following was appointed as the first viceroy of India by Queen Victoria?

(a) Robert Clive
(b) Lord Dalhousie
(c) Lord Canning
(d) Lord Wellesley

13. Complete the given analogy.
Biodegradable waste : Egg shells :: Non-biodegradable waste : ?

(a) Food waste (b) Grass
(c) Plants (d) Glass

14. Which of the following was the first holy book to be printed by a printing press?

(a) Bhagavad Geeta
(b) Bible
(c) Quran
(d) Guru Granth Sahib

15. Identify the logo of one of the special agencies of the United Nations with the help of picture given below.

(a) UNESCO (b) WHO
(c) UNICEF (d) ILO

16. ...... is the administrative organ of the United Nations which carries out the day to day work of the organisation.

(a) General Assembly
(b) Security Council
(c) Secretariat
(d) Economic and Social Council

17. Which among the following movement led by Mahatma Gandhi in the year 1921?

(a) Non-Cooperation Movement
(b) Civil Disobedience Movement
(c) Khilafat Movement
(d) Quit India Movement

18. The General Assembly appoints the UN Secretary-General on the recommendation of ....

(a) Secretariat
(b) Economic and Social Council
(c) Security Council
(d) International Court of Justice

19. Which of the following means of communication invented by Guglielmo Marconi?

(a) Internet
(b) Television
(c) Radio
(d) Satellite Communication

20. 'The Great Bath' is associated with which of the following Indus Valley sites?

(a) Dholavira (b) Harappa
(c) Lothal (d) Mohenjodaro

21. Who among the following is the head of a state?

(a) Chief Minister (b) President
(c) Governor (d) None of these

22. Name the movement from the given options, was started in response to the actions of disrespect by the British.

(a) Non-Cooperation Movement
(b) Quit India Movement
(c) Khilafat Movement
(d) Civil Disobedience Movement

23. Identify the name of a political party with the help of the picture given below.

(a) Communist Party of India
(b) Indian National Congress
(c) Samajwadi Party
(d) Bharatiya Janata Party

24. What is the basis of classification of temperature zones?

(a) Longitude (b) Latitude
(c) Hemispheres (d) Both (a) and (b)

25. Which among the following agricultural practices is considered as eco-friendly?

(a) Shifting cultivation
(b) Organic farming
(c) Subsistence farming
(d) Terrace farming

26. Who is associated with starting the journal Bande Mataram to expand revolutionary ideas of Indian Independence?

(a) Madam Bhikaji Cama
(b) Sarojini Naidu
(c) Aruna Asif Ali
(d) Sucheta Kriplani

27. Which neighbouring country of India shares its border with Jammu and Kashmir, Arunachal Pradesh, Uttarakhand, Sikkim and Himachal Pradesh?

(a) Nepal (b) Bhutan
(c) China (d) Myanmar

28. Ganpati Puja and Shivaji festival, to spread the message of nationalism and patriotism were started by ..... .

(a) Lala Lajpat Rai
(b) Bal Gangadhar Tilak
(c) Bipin Chandra Pal
(d) Surendranath Banerjee

29. What is/are the effect(s) of climate?

(a) It affects transportation.
(b) It affects housing and occupation.
(c) It affects food habits.
(d) All of the above

30. Who appoints the Judges of the Supreme Court in India?

(a) Governor (b) President
(c) Prime Minister (d) Chief Minister

31. .... is the network of intersecting parallels and meridians.

(a) Parallels
(b) Grid systems
(c) Latitudes
(d) Poles

32. Complete the given analogy.
Mangal Pandey : Meerut :: Bahadur Shah Zafar : ?

(a) Jhansi (b) Lucknow
(c) Delhi (d) Awadh

33. What is the fixed strength of Rajya Sabha of the Indian Parliament?

(a) 230 (b) 238
(c) 250 (d) 252

34. In which method, the entire solid waste is brought at one place and burnt. It is a very quick and easiest way to dispose the solid waste?

(a) Composting (b) Sanitary Landfills
(c) Incineration (d) Both (a) and (b)

35. Which of the following was not an outcome of the First War of Independence?

(a) Rule of East India Company came to an end.
(b) It promoted a sense of nationalism among people of India.
(c) India was directly governed by the British Queen.
(d) None of the above

36. What steps should be taken if there is a natural disaster like cyclone?

(a) One must stay away from windows.
(b) One must store food items in waterproof bags.
(c) One must try to drink only hot water.
(d) Both (a) and (b)

37. Why the seasons are caused on the Earth? Identify the reason from the given options.

(a) Earth rotates on its axis.
(b) Earth's axis is tilted as it moves around the Sun.
(c) The distance between Earth and Sun changes.
(d) None of the above

38. Who is associated with the invention of paper in 105 AD?

(a) Sumerians of Mesopotamia
(b) Johannes Gutenberg
(c) Egyptians
(d) Cai Lun of China

39. .... is appointed in the Union Territories holding the same rank as a Governor of a state.

(a) Lieutenant Governor
(b) Member of Parliament
(c) Chief Minister
(d) Council of Ministers of State

40. Which of the following UN agencies focuses on poverty reduction and the improvement of living standards worldwide?

(a) World Bank
(b) IMF
(c) WHO
(d) ILO

MCQs 2 Marks Questions

41. With reference to Stone age, which of the following is/are correct observation(s)?

I. Mesolithic Age may have started, when the agriculture began.
II. Neolithic people lived in more or less permanent habitations.

Choose the correct answer from the codes given below.

(a) Only I
(b) Only II
(c) Both I and II
(d) None of the above

42. Identify the incorrect pair with regards to historical events and related personalities given below.

(a) Lord Curzon – Partition of Bengal

(b) Sarojini Naidu – Non-Cooperation Movement

(c) Shaukat Ali – Khilafat Movement

(d) Rajguru – Civil Disobedience Movement

43. Read the given statements and select which ones are true (T) and which ones are false (F).

I. Delta is formed when river goes through the upper course stage.

II. An estuary is a small river that joins a big river.

Codes

	I	II
(a)	F	T
(b)	T	F
(c)	F	F
(d)	T	T

44. Identify the battle(s) from the description given below.

The East India Company started this battle against the combined army of the Nawabs of Bengal and Awadh and the Mughal Emperor Shah Alam. The British won the battle and obtained the Right to Collect Revenue in Bengal.

(a) Battle of Plassey

(b) Battle of Buxar

(c) Bengal War

(d) Both (a) and (b)

45. Choose the incorrect pair with regard to parallels of latitudes from the given options.

(a) 23 ½ ° N latitude – Tropic of Cancer

(b) 23 ½ ° S latitude – Greenwich

(c) 66 ½ ° N latitude – Arctic Circle

(d) 66 ½ ° S latitude – Antarctic Circle

46. Match the following.

	List I (Inventions/ Discoveries)	List II (Associated Personalities)
A.	Radio	1. James Watt
B.	Steam Engine	2. Marconi
C.	Pasteurisation	3. Alexander Fleming
D.	Pencillin	4. Louis Pasteur

Codes

	A	B	C	D
(a)	2	1	4	3
(b)	1	3	4	2
(c)	4	2	3	1
(d)	3	1	2	4

47. Read the given statements and select which ones are true (T) and which ones are false (F).

I. Mahatma Gandhi returned from South Africa in 1920 and joined the National Movement.

II. Mahatma Gandhi believed that only violent methods would force the Britishers to leave India.

Codes

	I	II		I	II
(a)	T	T	(b)	F	F
(c)	T	F	(d)	F	T

48. **Identify the Union Territory marked as 'A' in the given map of India.**

(a) Puducherry
(b) Daman and Diu
(c) Lakshadweep
(d) Andaman and Nicobar Islands

49. **Consider the following statements and choose the correct one from the given options.**

I. Oceans heat up and cool down slower than the land around them.

II. The climate of a place is greatly influenced by its distance from the equator.

Codes
(a) Only I
(b) Both I and II
(c) Only II
(d) None of the above

50. **Match the following.**

List I		List II	
A.	UNICEF	1.	1945
B.	UNESCO	2.	1919
C.	WHO	3.	1948
D.	ILO	4.	1946

Codes

	A	B	C	D
(a)	4	3	2	1
(b)	4	1	3	2
(c)	3	4	1	2
(d)	2	3	4	1

Darken your choice with HB Pencil

1.	ⓐ ⓑ ⓒ ⓓ	10.	ⓐ ⓑ ⓒ ⓓ	19.	ⓐ ⓑ ⓒ ⓓ	28.	ⓐ ⓑ ⓒ ⓓ	37.	ⓐ ⓑ ⓒ ⓓ	46.	ⓐ ⓑ ⓒ ⓓ
2.	ⓐ ⓑ ⓒ ⓓ	11.	ⓐ ⓑ ⓒ ⓓ	20.	ⓐ ⓑ ⓒ ⓓ	29.	ⓐ ⓑ ⓒ ⓓ	38.	ⓐ ⓑ ⓒ ⓓ	47.	ⓐ ⓑ ⓒ ⓓ
3.	ⓐ ⓑ ⓒ ⓓ	12.	ⓐ ⓑ ⓒ ⓓ	21.	ⓐ ⓑ ⓒ ⓓ	30.	ⓐ ⓑ ⓒ ⓓ	39.	ⓐ ⓑ ⓒ ⓓ	48.	ⓐ ⓑ ⓒ ⓓ
4.	ⓐ ⓑ ⓒ ⓓ	13.	ⓐ ⓑ ⓒ ⓓ	22.	ⓐ ⓑ ⓒ ⓓ	31.	ⓐ ⓑ ⓒ ⓓ	40.	ⓐ ⓑ ⓒ ⓓ	49.	ⓐ ⓑ ⓒ ⓓ
5.	ⓐ ⓑ ⓒ ⓓ	14.	ⓐ ⓑ ⓒ ⓓ	23.	ⓐ ⓑ ⓒ ⓓ	32.	ⓐ ⓑ ⓒ ⓓ	41.	ⓐ ⓑ ⓒ ⓓ	50.	ⓐ ⓑ ⓒ ⓓ
6.	ⓐ ⓑ ⓒ ⓓ	15.	ⓐ ⓑ ⓒ ⓓ	24.	ⓐ ⓑ ⓒ ⓓ	33.	ⓐ ⓑ ⓒ ⓓ	42.	ⓐ ⓑ ⓒ ⓓ		
7.	ⓐ ⓑ ⓒ ⓓ	16.	ⓐ ⓑ ⓒ ⓓ	25.	ⓐ ⓑ ⓒ ⓓ	34.	ⓐ ⓑ ⓒ ⓓ	43.	ⓐ ⓑ ⓒ ⓓ		
8.	ⓐ ⓑ ⓒ ⓓ	17.	ⓐ ⓑ ⓒ ⓓ	26.	ⓐ ⓑ ⓒ ⓓ	35.	ⓐ ⓑ ⓒ ⓓ	44.	ⓐ ⓑ ⓒ ⓓ		
9.	ⓐ ⓑ ⓒ ⓓ	18.	ⓐ ⓑ ⓒ ⓓ	27.	ⓐ ⓑ ⓒ ⓓ	36.	ⓐ ⓑ ⓒ ⓓ	45.	ⓐ ⓑ ⓒ ⓓ		

Practice Set 02

Time : 60 Mins. Max. Marks : 60

General Instructions

1. This question paper contains 50 questions.
2. All questions are compulsory. There is no negative marking.
3. This question paper is divided into two parts; In Part I, there are 40 MCQs of 1 mark each while in Part II, there are 10 MCQs of 2 marks each.
4. Use HB pencil / Blue ball point pen to mark your choice of answer by darkening the circles on the OMR Sheet.

MCQs 1 Mark Questions

1. Who is indirectly elected by the people through elected members of the Parliament of India and the Legislative Assemblies of the States?

(a) Prime Minister (b) President
(c) Chief minister (d) None of these

2. Which of the following is/are the site(s) in the Indus Valley Civilisation?

(a) Lothal (b) Harappa
(c) Kalibangan (d) All of these

3. In India, political parties are given recognition by ....

(a) Election Commission
(b) Speaker of Lok Sabha
(c) President
(d) Supreme Court

4. Which of the following is the largest state (area wise) in India?

(a) Uttar Pradesh (b) Rajasthan
(c) Madhya Pradesh (d) West Bengal

5. Who among the following leaders belonged to the moderate group of leaders?

(a) Bal Gangadhar Tilak
(b) Gopal Krishna Gokhale
(c) Lala Lajpat Rai
(d) Bipin Chandra Pal

6. Identify the type of industry from the given image and choose the correct option.

(a) Iron and Steel Industry
(b) Oil and Petroleum Industry
(c) Food Industry
(d) Cement Industry

7. Which was the first metal discovered by man?

(a) Bronze (b) Silver
(c) Iron (d) Copper

8. Which among the following soils is not suitable for agriculture purpose?

(a) Alluvial soil (b) Red soil
(c) Mountain soil (d) Desert soil

9. What does the term 'Secular' mean in the Indian context?

(a) All religions are equal in the eyes of the government.

(b) Special importance to a religion related to minorities.

(c) One religion is promoted by the government.

(d) None of the above

10. Identify the famous moderate leader from the given image.

(a) Bal Gangadhar Tilak

(b) Bipin Chandra Pal

(c) Lala Lajpat Rai

(d) Dadabhai Naoroji

11. Which among the following food crop occupies the largest part of the cropped area in India?

(a) Wheat (b) Millets

(c) Rice (d) Pulses

12. What was the symbol of the Swadeshi Movement?

(a) Lotus and Bread

(b) Spinning Wheel

(c) Hammer and Sickle

(d) None of the above

13. Identify the agency of United Nations with the help of the given logo.

(a) UNESCO (b) WHO

(c) ILO (d) FAO

14. Who exercises the actual executive power under the Parliamentary form of government?

(a) President (b) Prime Minister

(c) Supreme Court (d) Bureaucracy

15. The continents and ocean floor, together form the .... of the Earth.

(a) outer core (b) inner core

(c) crust (d) mantle

16. Which of the following scripts was used during the Indus Valley Civilisation?

(a) Brahmi script (b) Devanagari script

(c) Dravidian script (d) None of these

17. The non-permanent members of Security Council are elected for a period of .... years.

(a) 2 (b) 3 (c) 4 (d) 5

18. What is/are the importance of Plains?

(a) They are great tourist attraction.

(b) They are fertile and productive.

(c) They are most suitable for habitation.

(d) Both (b) and (c)

19. Which of the following is the world's largest river island, located in Assam?

(a) Ganga (b) Yamuna
(c) Majuli (d) Godavari

20. What is the official term of the President's office?

(a) 4 years (b) 5 years
(c) 6 years (d) None of these

21. Which of the following is the highest plateau in the world?

(a) Deccan Plateau (b) Mexican Plateau
(c) Plateau of Tibet (d) Colorado Plateau

22. Who among the following gave the slogan 'Delhi Chalo'?

(a) Mahatma Gandhi
(b) Subhash Chandra Bose
(c) Mohan Singh
(d) Jawaharlal Nehru

23. Which of the following is not a main organ of United Nations?

(a) International Court of Justice
(b) Economic and Social Council
(c) Secretariat
(d) International Monetary Fund

24. APJ Abdul Kalam was responsible for the development of which of the following missiles?

(a) AGNI (b) PRITHVI
(c) AKASH (d) Both (a) and (b)

25. The total number of members represented in General Assembly is ....

(a) 191 (b) 193
(c) 195 (d) 197

26. What is/are the sources found from Neolithic site of Burzahom in Jammu and Kashmir?

(a) Presence of polished stone tools.
(b) Practice of burial of dogs along with their masters.
(c) Both (a) and (b)
(d) None of the above

27. Which of the following is not a greenhouse gas?

(a) Carbon dioxide (b) Methane
(c) Nitrous oxide (d) Carbon monoxide

28. Identify the UN agency that focus on poverty reduction and the improvement of living standards worldwide.

(a) World Bank (b) IMF
(c) WHO (d) ILO

29. How many judges are there within the International Court of Justice?

(a) 9 judges (b) 11 judges
(c) 14 judges (d) 15 judges

30. The personality given in the picture below is related to which historical event?

(a) Partition of Bengal
(b) Establishment of the Indian National Congress
(c) Dandi March
(d) Quit India Movement

31. If the latitude of a place is 30° N, it lies in the ....

(a) Tropical Zone
(b) North Temperate Zone
(c) Frigid Zone
(d) South Temperate Zone

32. Who was known as the 'Father of Modern India' and was a great social reformer?

(a) CV Raman
(b) Raja Ram Mohan Roy
(c) Homi Jehangir Bhabha
(d) Rabindranath Tagore

33. According to the Preamble, from where does the Constitution derives its authority?

(a) Indian Culture
(b) Government of India
(c) The People of India
(d) Princely states

34. The first railway network in India was built between .... in 1853.

(a) Ahmedabad to Gandhinagar
(b) Mumbai to Pune
(c) Mumbai to Thane
(d) Delhi to Agra

35. What was the reason behind the failure of 1857 revolt?

(a) Due to the superior resources of the British Empire.
(b) It was poorly organised and the rebels had no common ideal.
(c) It had very little nationalist sentiment.
(d) None of the above

36. Global warming is caused due to the emission of ....

(a) Nitrogen (b) Carbon dioxide
(c) Carbon Monoxide (d) Sulphur dioxide

37. Complete the given analogy from the given options.
Largest Continent : Asia :: Smallest Continent : ?

(a) Australia (b) North America
(c) South America (d) Africa

38. Why deforestation causes soil erosion faster? Identify the reason from the given options.

(a) Roots absorb water.
(b) Roots absorb minerals.
(c) Roots provide nutrients.
(d) Roots hold the soil firmly.

39. ...... reduces the use of raw materials that would have been used.

(a) Recycling
(b) Reusing
(c) Both (a) and (b)
(d) Reducing the waste

40. Identify the powerful leader of the freedom struggle who left Congress and formed the Indian National Army in 1941, to fight against the British.

(a) Bal Gangadhar Tilak
(b) Netaji Subhash Chandra Bose
(c) Khan Abdul Ghaffar Khan
(d) Motilal Nehru

MCQs 2 Marks Questions

41. Read the given statements and select which ones are true (T) and which ones are false (F).

I. The first British factory was set up in Surat in 1608.
II. The British policy of fort building was opposed by Mughal Emperor Shah Alam II.

	I	II		I	II
(a)	F	F	(b)	T	F
(c)	F	T	(d)	T	T

42. Consider the following statements and choose the correct ones from the given options.

I. The Election Commission of India ensures that free and fair elections are held in the country.

II. The President is the real Head of the country.

Which of the following statements is/are correct?

(a) Only I (b) Both I and II

(c) Only II (d) None of these

43. Choose the incorrect pair from the given options.

(a) International Labour Organisation – Geneva, Switzerland

(b) World Bank – Washington DC, USA

(c) International Court of Justice – The Hague, Netherlands

(d) UNESCO – New York, USA

44. Match the following.

List I	List II
A. Hills	1. Vast stretches of flat, mainly grassy areas
B. Plateau	2. Lowland between two mountains
C. Valley	3. A mountain with a flat top.
D. Plains	4. Higher elevations on the Earth's surface with a distinct peak.

Codes

	A	B	C	D
(a)	2	3	4	1
(b)	3	4	1	2
(c)	4	3	2	1
(d)	1	2	3	4

45. Identify the personality with the help of given source of information.

He is the elected head of the Council of Ministers in a state. He is the leader of the majority party in the Vidhan Sabha.

(a) Governor

(b) Lieutenant Governor

(c) Chief Minister

(d) Member of Legislative Assembly

46. Choose the correct pair of colours which are used as symbols on a map to share information from the given options.

(a) White — Water Bodies

(b) Yellow — Deserts

(c) Green — Plateaus

(d) Black — Mountains

47. Match the following pairs correctly.

	List I (Leader)		List II (Centre of Revolt)
A.	Kunwar Singh	1.	Kanpur
B.	Nana Saheb	2.	Delhi
C.	Begum Hazrat Mahal	3.	Jagdishpur
D.	Bahadur Shah Zafar	4.	Lucknow

Codes

	A	B	C	D
(a)	3	1	4	2
(b)	4	3	2	1
(c)	1	2	3	4
(d)	2	4	1	3

48. **Read the given statements and select which ones are true (T) and which ones are false (F).**

I. India was one of the first 50 nations, who signed the UN Charter on 24th October, 1945.

II. General Assembly is the most important organ and the main body of the United Nations.

Codes

	I	II		I	II
(a)	T	T	(b)	F	F
(c)	F	T	(d)	T	F

49. **Consider the following statements**

I. Seismograph is a device used to measure the intensity of earthquake.

II. Maximum vibrations are felt far from the epicentre during an earthquake.

Which of the following statements is/are incorrect?

(a) Only I (b) Only II
(c) Both I and II (d) Neither I nor II

50. **Which of the following movements started as a result of activities associated with the state shaded in the map given below?**

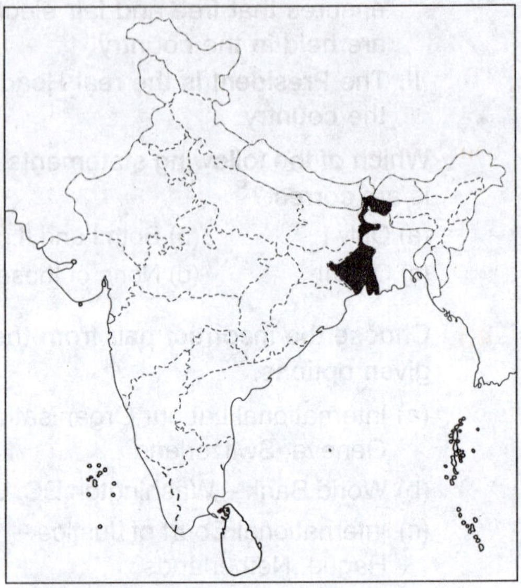

(a) Non-Cooperation Movement
(b) Swadeshi and Boycott Movements
(c) Civil Disobedience Movement
(d) Quit India Movement

Darken your choice with HB Pencil

1. ⓐ ⓑ ⓒ ⓓ	10. ⓐ ⓑ ⓒ ⓓ	19. ⓐ ⓑ ⓒ ⓓ	28. ⓐ ⓑ ⓒ ⓓ	37. ⓐ ⓑ ⓒ ⓓ	46. ⓐ ⓑ ⓒ ⓓ
2. ⓐ ⓑ ⓒ ⓓ	11. ⓐ ⓑ ⓒ ⓓ	20. ⓐ ⓑ ⓒ ⓓ	29. ⓐ ⓑ ⓒ ⓓ	38. ⓐ ⓑ ⓒ ⓓ	47. ⓐ ⓑ ⓒ ⓓ
3. ⓐ ⓑ ⓒ ⓓ	12. ⓐ ⓑ ⓒ ⓓ	21. ⓐ ⓑ ⓒ ⓓ	30. ⓐ ⓑ ⓒ ⓓ	39. ⓐ ⓑ ⓒ ⓓ	48. ⓐ ⓑ ⓒ ⓓ
4. ⓐ ⓑ ⓒ ⓓ	13. ⓐ ⓑ ⓒ ⓓ	22. ⓐ ⓑ ⓒ ⓓ	31. ⓐ ⓑ ⓒ ⓓ	40. ⓐ ⓑ ⓒ ⓓ	49. ⓐ ⓑ ⓒ ⓓ
5. ⓐ ⓑ ⓒ ⓓ	14. ⓐ ⓑ ⓒ ⓓ	23. ⓐ ⓑ ⓒ ⓓ	32. ⓐ ⓑ ⓒ ⓓ	41. ⓐ ⓑ ⓒ ⓓ	50. ⓐ ⓑ ⓒ ⓓ
6. ⓐ ⓑ ⓒ ⓓ	15. ⓐ ⓑ ⓒ ⓓ	24. ⓐ ⓑ ⓒ ⓓ	33. ⓐ ⓑ ⓒ ⓓ	42. ⓐ ⓑ ⓒ ⓓ	
7. ⓐ ⓑ ⓒ ⓓ	16. ⓐ ⓑ ⓒ ⓓ	25. ⓐ ⓑ ⓒ ⓓ	34. ⓐ ⓑ ⓒ ⓓ	43. ⓐ ⓑ ⓒ ⓓ	
8. ⓐ ⓑ ⓒ ⓓ	17. ⓐ ⓑ ⓒ ⓓ	26. ⓐ ⓑ ⓒ ⓓ	35. ⓐ ⓑ ⓒ ⓓ	44. ⓐ ⓑ ⓒ ⓓ	
9. ⓐ ⓑ ⓒ ⓓ	18. ⓐ ⓑ ⓒ ⓓ	27. ⓐ ⓑ ⓒ ⓓ	36. ⓐ ⓑ ⓒ ⓓ	45. ⓐ ⓑ ⓒ ⓓ	

Answer Sheet

Chapter 01

1. (a)	**2.** (b)	**3.** (c)	**4.** (b)	**5.** (c)	**6.** (d)	**7.** (b)	**8.** (c)	**9.** (b)	**10.** (a)
11. (a)	**12.** (c)	**13.** (c)	**14.** (a)	**15.** (c)	**16.** (c)	**17.** (b)	**18.** (b)	**19.** (a)	**20.** (a)
21. (a)	**22.** (a)	**23.** (b)	**24.** (a)	**25.** (a)	**26.** (c)				

Chapter 02

1. (b)	**2.** (b)	**3.** (d)	**4.** (a)	**5.** (c)	**6.** (d)	**7.** (d)	**8.** (b)	**9.** (b)	**10.** (a)
11. (b)	**12.** (d)	**13.** (b)	**14.** (a)	**15.** (b)	**16.** (d)	**17.** (d)	**18.** (b)	**19.** (c)	**20.** (c)
21. (b)	**22.** (a)	**23.** (c)	**24.** (a)	**25.** (c)					

Chapter 03

1. (c)	**2.** (c)	**3.** (a)	**4.** (a)	**5.** (d)	**6.** (a)	**7.** (a)	**8.** (a)	**9.** (c)	**10.** (b)
11. (a)	**12.** (b)	**13.** (a)	**14.** (c)	**15.** (c)	**16.** (a)	**17.** (d)	**18.** (b)	**19.** (a)	**20.** (c)
21. (b)	**22.** (c)	**23.** (c)							

Chapter 04

1. (b)	**2.** (d)	**3.** (c)	**4.** (a)	**5.** (a)	**6.** (a)	**7.** (b)	**8.** (d)	**9.** (b)	**10.** (c)
11. (c)	**12.** (a)	**13.** (b)	**14.** (b)	**15.** (c)	**16.** (c)	**17.** (a)	**18.** (b)	**19.** (a)	**20.** (a)
21. (b)	**22.** (c)	**23.** (a)	**24.** (d)	**25.** (a)	**26.** (b)	**27.** (d)			

Chapter 05

1. (c)	**2.** (a)	**3.** (a)	**4.** (b)	**5.** (b)	**6.** (b)	**7.** (a)	**8.** (b)	**9.** (c)	**10.** (b)
11. (a)	**12.** (a)	**13.** (a)	**14.** (b)	**15.** (b)	**16.** (c)	**17.** (c)	**18.** (b)	**19.** (b)	**20.** (c)
21. (b)	**22.** (a)	**23.** (b)	**24.** (a)	**25.** (d)	**26.** (c)	**27.** (a)			

Chapter 06

1. (b)	**2.** (a)	**3.** (a)	**4.** (d)	**5.** (c)	**6.** (a)	**7.** (b)	**8.** (a)	**9.** (b)	**10.** (b)
11. (a)	**12.** (a)	**13.** (a)	**14.** (b)	**15.** (b)	**16.** (c)	**17.** (b)	**18.** (b)	**19.** (c)	**20.** (d)
21. (c)	**22.** (c)	**23.** (a)	**24.** (d)						

Chapter 07

1. (d)	**2.** (b)	**3.** (a)	**4.** (c)	**5.** (d)	**6.** (b)	**7.** (c)	**8.** (c)	**9.** (c)	**10.** (b)
11. (b)	**12.** (b)	**13.** (a)	**14.** (a)	**15.** (b)	**16.** (d)	**17.** (b)	**18.** (c)	**19.** (c)	**20.** (c)
21. (c)	**22.** (a)	**23.** (d)							

Chapter 08

1. (c)	2. (a)	3. (c)	4. (d)	5. (b)	6. (c)	7. (d)	8. (c)	9. (b)	10. (b)
11. (d)	12. (b)	13. (c)	14. (a)	15. (a)	16. (d)	17. (c)	18. (c)	19. (c)	20. (a)
21. (c)	22. (b)								

Chapter 09

1. (d)	2. (a)	3. (b)	4. (c)	5. (d)	6. (c)	7. (d)	8. (b)	9. (b)	10. (b)
11. (c)	12. (b)	13. (a)	14. (d)	15. (d)	16. (a)	17. (c)	18. (d)	19. (d)	20. (b)
21. (c)	22. (b)	23. (a)	24. (c)	25. (d)					

Chapter 10

1. (a)	2. (a)	3. (b)	4. (b)	5. (b)	6. (a)	7. (c)	8. (b)	9. (b)	10. (d)
11. (c)	12. (a)	13. (d)	14. (a)	15. (a)	16. (a)	17. (b)	18. (d)	19. (c)	20. (a)
21. (c)	22. (a)	23. (b)	24. (a)	25. (c)	26. (a)				

Chapter 11

1. (b)	2. (a)	3. (b)	4. (b)	5. (b)	6. (d)	7. (c)	8. (b)	9. (a)	10. (a)
11. (b)	12. (d)	13. (c)	14. (c)	15. (a)	16. (a)	17. (a)	18. (d)	19. (c)	20. (a)
21. (b)	22. (d)	23. (b)	24. (a)	25. (d)					

Chapter 12

1. (b)	2. (b)	3. (b)	4. (b)	5. (a)	6. (a)	7. (a)	8. (a)	9. (a)	10. (c)
11. (a)	12. (b)	13. (a)	14. (b)	15. (d)	16. (c)	17. (c)	18. (b)	19. (d)	20. (c)
21. (a)	22. (d)								

Practice Set 01

1. (d)	2. (d)	3. (a)	4. (c)	5. (c)	6. (a)	7. (a)	8. (c)	9. (b)	10. (a)
11. (d)	12. (c)	13. (d)	14. (b)	15. (c)	16. (c)	17. (a)	18. (c)	19. (c)	20. (d)
21. (c)	22. (c)	23. (a)	24. (b)	25. (b)	26. (a)	27. (c)	28. (b)	29. (d)	30. (b)
31. (b)	32. (c)	33. (c)	34. (c)	35. (d)	36. (d)	37. (b)	38. (d)	39. (a)	40. (a)
41. (b)	42. (d)	43. (c)	44. (b)	45. (b)	46. (a)	47. (b)	48. (a)	49. (b)	50. (b)

Practice Set 02

1. (b)	2. (d)	3. (a)	4. (b)	5. (b)	6. (b)	7. (d)	8. (d)	9. (a)	10. (d)
11. (c)	12. (b)	13. (b)	14. (b)	15. (c)	16. (d)	17. (a)	18. (d)	19. (c)	20. (b)
21. (c)	22. (b)	23. (d)	24. (d)	25. (b)	26. (c)	27. (d)	28. (a)	29. (d)	30. (b)
31. (b)	32. (b)	33. (c)	34. (c)	35. (b)	36. (b)	37. (a)	38. (d)	39. (a)	40. (b)
41. (b)	42. (a)	43. (d)	44. (c)	45. (c)	46. (b)	47. (a)	48. (a)	49. (b)	50. (b)